D1211315

STRANGE POWERS

COLIN WILSON

STRANGE POWERS

VINTAGE BOOKS

A Division of Random House

New York

FIRST VINTAGE BOOKS EDITION, February 1976

Copyright © 1973 by Colin Wilson (Publications) Ltd.

Library of Congress Cataloging in Publication Data

Wilson, Colin, 1931–
    Strange Powers.

    1. Leftwich, Robert.   2. Beattle, Eunice.   3. Guirdham,
Arthur.   4. Psychical research—Biography.   5. Occult sci-
ences—Biography.   I. Title.
[BF1026.W53 1976]   133.9′0922   75-28138
ISBN 0-394-71947-6
Manufactured in the United States of America

CONTENTS

STRANGE
POWERS

INTRODUCTION

The writer finds very considerable reason for believing that, within a period to be estimated by weeks and months rather than by aeons, there has been a fundamental change in the conditions under which life, not simply human life but all self-conscious existence, has been going on since its beginning.

With these strange words, H. G. Wells began his final book *Mind at the End of Its Tether*, written in 1945, the year before his death. It sounded like one of the Jehovah's Witnesses' doomsday prophecies. 'The end of everything we call life is at hand,' said Wells, 'and cannot be evaded.' In the quarter of a century that has passed since his death, there has been no obvious sign of the 'fundamental change' that Wells foresaw. But no, that is not quite true. There *has* been a change, and a very important one: not in the conditions of life, but in the attitude of the civilised western mind to those conditions. It is a change that would have amazed Wells, and perhaps irritated him. For although Wells could not have known it, he died in the last decade before the end of scientific determinism. This determinism—the belief that the universe is basically a machine, and that life is just a highly complicated mechanical process—had reigned supreme for more than a century, and it seemed to have come to stay. Its basic attitude could be summarised like this. 'Man has always been infinitely capable of error and self-deception. Now he has found a method that can save him from them—the scientific method. He must clear his mind of all preconceptions, and then merely face the *facts*. Concentrate entirely on facts, and on drawing rational conclusions from those facts. . . .' It was a creed to which Wells subscribed without reservation, and he could not conceive that it might ever be changed or modified—unless the human mind should plunge again into the errors of the dark ages. It was the creed that finally led him to the despair of *Mind at the End of Its Tether*, with its feeling that man is a hopeless, incorrigible self-deceiver who is due for a brutal awakening. . . . Victorian science said man had no right to false hope; Wells said man had no right to hope at all. He was saying that the human mind is so full of its own importance that it cannot get used to the idea that it is *totally* unimportant; worse than unimportant—negligible, almost non-existent. Wells had taken the 'scientific attitude' as far as it would go; the pendulum had to start swinging in the opposite direction. . . .

It did—although the first signs of it would have struck Wells as absurd, a sign of decadence. I had come to London, at the age of twenty, in 1951, and I noticed, in bookshops in the Charing Cross Road, books with titles like *A Buddhist Bible*, *The Myth of the Magus*, *Tibet's Great Yogi Milarepa*, the *I Ching*, *In Search of the Miraculous*, *Worlds in Collision*. Now my own training, insofar as I'd had any, had been scientific, and I was very much of Wells's way of thinking. I understood that the scientific attitude is not basically just a spoilsport scepticism. T. H. Huxley defined the scientific attitude as 'sitting down before the facts like a little child,' and following wherever they lead. And I knew that this attitude can bring an almost mystical sensation of opening vistas, a universe full of extraordinary facts, all waiting to be absorbed into the realm of human knowledge. But there are all kinds of facts and truths: historical, philosophical, literary, legal, religious, and I saw no reason to limit my interest to the kind of facts that Wells regarded as the scientist's proper province. So I borrowed the *I Ching* and the *Malleus Maleficarum* and *Tibetan Book of the Dead* and books by Montague Summers on witches and vampires from the library. And it soon struck me that there is a problem here that Wells had never taken the trouble to define. For example, Immanuel Velikovsky's best-seller *Worlds in Collision* is certainly a crank book; but not because he believes that a giant comet from Jupiter caused tidal upheavals and gave rise to such phenomena as the fall of the walls of Jericho and the parting of the Red Sea to let the Israelites through. From the scientific point of view, *Worlds in Collision* and *Ages in Chaos* are full of interesting facts about some strange catastrophe that tore mammoths and mastodons limb from limb and then buried them in black mud, about giant boulders in the Jura mountains apparently torn from the Alps. Frozen mammoths have been found that must have been frozen almost instantaneously, for there has been no decay of inner tissues (they are still edible when unfrozen). Any modern cold storage firm will tell you that this is almost impossible for a creature of that size. To begin with, unless it is frozen very rapidly, the crystals of ice that form are so large that they burst the cells of the tissues, and the meat loses flavour when unfrozen; the Beresovka mammoth was frozen so rapidly that only the tiniest crystals formed throughout.* *Some* catastrophe happened very suddenly indeed, and it is the business of science to try to explain it. On the other hand, there is no real evidence to link these prehistoric mysteries with the fall of the walls of Jericho when the Israelites blew their trumpets. Velikovsky is a crank because he reasons badly and wrongly from his facts—not because there is something wrong with the facts themselves. But a scientist who declined to read Velikovsky on the grounds that he is a crank would also be guilty of prejudiced thinking. Velikovsky's reasoning may be shaky; but the facts remain. And it is not his preoccupation with these strange facts that makes Velikovsky a crank. There is an emotional prejudice behind the choice of 'the facts' the scientist is willing to take seriously: a feeling that certain facts are 'good taste' and certain others are bad taste. Quite unconsciously, he has come to limit his interest to the kind of facts that fit into the kind of jigsaw puzzle he is good at solving.

I was clearly aware of this as I read the *I Ching* or Ouspensky's *New Model of the Universe*. The idea of throwing down coins to learn about the future is absurd and indefensible from the Wellsian point of view. On the other hand, like everybody else, I had observed the way that coincidences *do* sometimes form odd patterns. I can offer an example that occurred only a few days before writing these pages. Reading a review of a recording of Verdi's early opera *Attila*, I saw a reference to a ballet called *The Lady and the Fool,* put together from early Verdi operas. I found this record on my shelves— I didn't know I had it, and had certainly never played it—and discovered that the ballet had been arranged by

* The mystery of the frozen mammoths—with buttercups in their stomachs—is discussed by Ivan Sanderson in a *Saturday Evening Post* article of 1960, reprinted in *More Things* (1969).

John Cranko. The record notes mentioned that Cranko's other most popular ballet was *Pineapple Poll,* arranged from the music of Arthur Sullivan. I knew I had this, so I took it out, and played it after I had played *The Lady and the Fool.* At half past eight in the evening—immediately after playing the records—there was a programme I wanted to listen to on the radio; I switched on at 8.25. The radio happened to be tuned to the wrong station, and a news-reader was announcing the death that day of John Cranko, whose best-known ballets were *The Lady and the Fool* and *Pineapple Poll.* Not a tremendously exciting coincidence, I agree. But odd. I had probably possessed the record of *The Lady and the Fool* for years but never played it; I hadn't played *Pineapple Poll* for years either, and didn't know it was by Cranko. These were the only two records I played during the evening before hearing the news of his death.

Wells would say: Very well, what conclusion do you draw from that? That some invisible intelligence wanted to direct your attention to Cranko? Perhaps Cranko's ghost? Or that there was some mysterious working of providence . . . ? No, I am not suggesting either of these. I merely observe that coincidences of this sort happen sufficiently often to suggest that they shouldn't be ignored. Science consists basically of observation of events that are repeated—whether it is the sun rising every morning, or a comet returning every hundred and fifty years. This is no place to discuss Jung's idea of synchronicity—I will do so later; at the moment, I would only say that if a 'chance' occurs often enough, the chance of it being pure chance soon becomes unlikely. I also note, in passing, that these coincidences seem to occur more often when I am psychologically healthy than when I'm tired or depressed—perhaps suggesting that some unconscious radar-system is in operation.

As to Ouspensky—and his teacher Gurdjieff: they raise the question of crankery in a very clear form. Half Gurdjieff's 'system' consists of psychological observations of an acuteness that amounts to genius; he is on the same level as Kierkegaard, Nietzsche and William James. The other half consists of strang assertions about planetary levels, the 'ray of creation' and tables of 'hydrogens' that are unknown to chemistry. This part of the system may have profound occult meanings, or it may be a home-made symbolism, like the mythical personalities of Blake's Prophetic Books. A highly intelligent friend of mine—and one of the most intelligent men I have ever known—dismissed Gurdjieff as a complete crank and charlatan; he was a humanistic philosopher rather than a scientist; but he was, it seems to me, slipping into the same 'fallacy of intolerance' as Wells. Gurdjieff did not suit his preconceived idea of the rational and logical; so he let his emotions guide his reason, and dismissed him.

The problem is that the humanistic rationalist blinds himself in *complete good faith*. To keep a genuinely open mind is a matter of tremendous difficulty. We can slip into a 'point of view' that imposes rigid patterns on everything we see, and which makes certain things inconceivable. You only recognise it as a mental straitjacket when you have got rid of it. For example, although I read Montague Summers's *History of Witchcraft* with pleasure, it seemed self-evident to me that he was a crank or a liar. No sensible person, writing in the age of Einstein and Planck, could believe that 'black witches' were really wicked, and that they possessed real powers. Summers undoubtedly was a bit of a crank and a bit of a *poseur;* so it seemed fairly clear that he was pretending to believe in witchcraft to give his book a

'new angle.' * Nearly twenty years later, when writing
The Occult, I took basically the same view. So, for example, when writing of the curious case of the North
Berwick witches, executed in 1591 for raising a storm in
which they tried to drown the king, I took it for granted
that it was basically a case of hysteria, superstition and
credulity. Yet elsewhere in the same book, I accept evidence that African witch doctors can summon rain. (To
begin with, it had been described to me by two friends
who had actually seen it: Negley Farson and Martin
Delaney.) It only struck me some time afterwards that I
was being illogical in *taking it for granted* that the North
Berwick witches were innocent. *Some* aspects of the
case are very odd. At one point in the examination,
King James I declared the whole thing was a tissue of
nonsense. Whereupon one of the chief accused, Agnes
Sampson, drew him aside and whispered in his ear certain words that he had spoken to his bride, Anne of
Denmark, on their wedding night when they were alone;
no one but the king and his bride knew them. The king
was immediately convinced that he was dealing with real
witches. Why should Agnes Sampson have done this,
when James was in a mood to dismiss the whole thing as
imagination? The account of the case given by Rossell
Hope Robbins in his *Encyclopedia of Witchcraft and
Demonology* (1959) takes it for granted that all were
innocent, and praises the courage of the schoolmaster,
John Fian, who confessed after torture, but later with-
drew his confession and died asserting his innocence.
But Robbins fails to mention the important fact that
Fian was the secretary of the Earl of Bothwell—who, in
later life, had the reputation of being a dabbler in black
magic, and who had every reason to intrigue against his
cousin the king. When the king was sailing back from

* He succeeded; it was a best-seller.

Denmark with his newly married bride, a tremendous storm arose and almost sank the ship; the witches confessed to raising this storm, with Fian's help. Neither does he mention that, on the morning after his confession, Fian told his jailers, without prompting, that he had been visited by the devil during the night. Robbins explains the confession by emphasising how horribly Fian was tortured, his leg crushed by 'the boot'; yet Fian escaped twenty-four hours later, and managed to get back home. (So Robbins is forced to the conclusion that the escape was mythical, inserted by the chronicler to heighten the effect of the story.)

Robbins could be right. But there is another interpretation. There is evidence that Bothwell was plotting to kill the king, whom he hoped to supplant on the throne of England. Fian was his secretary. Suppose Fian *was* responsible for ceremonies to try to raise a storm to wreck the king's ship? Suppose the witches were not just self-deluding old hags, but possessed the same power as African witch doctors? Suppose Agnes Sampson had some genuine extra-sensory knowledge of what passed between the king and his bride on their wedding night and, having once committed herself to confession and repentance, decided to use this knowledge to convince the king when he became sceptical . . . ? This version fits the facts as well as Robbins's 'martyrdom of the innocent' theory. In fact, rather better.

Having reached this conclusion, it struck me that I was now appreciably closer to the position of Montague Summers, and that he might not be as dishonest as I had assumed. Summers does not deny that many innocent women have been executed as witches; he only argues that there *is* a tradition of 'black witchcraft' in Europe. I cannot go along with him in believing that witches really summoned the devil—although I would accept that they might have summoned 'powers of evil,' whatever that means. The truth probably lies somewhere midway between Summers's total acceptance of black witchcraft and Robbins's total scepticism.

As far as magic and occultism went, I remained basically a sceptic. But in *The Outsider*, which I started to write over Christmas 1954, I expressed my revulsion from the determinism and reductionism of modern science. (For example, I had always disliked Freud's attempt to explain Moses, Leonardo and Dostoevsky in terms of Oedipus complexes, castration fears, etc.) In *The Outsider* and *Religion and the Rebel*, I was more concerned with the problem from a philosophical angle: that two of the most influential modern philosophical movements, logical positivism and linguistic analysis, should regard questions of human freedom as more or less meaningless. With Heidegger and Sartre, I accepted that man is capable of expressing free will—and therefore of some non-religious version of 'damnation' and 'salvation.' Having worked in factories, offices, restaurants, I had a highly developed sense of the futility of certain modes of activity, and also of the strong feeling of meaning and freedom in others—for example, in self-expression (in my case, through writing), in travel, in romantic or sexual involvements. As far as I was concerned, a life spent in menial jobs was a form of damnation; while Rupert Brooke's lines about a smell

> . . . that fills
> The soul with longing for dim hills
> And far horizons

brought a taste of freedom, of meaning, of 'salvation.' It was no good telling me that these words express linguistic misunderstandings.

But at the time *The Outsider* came out, in 1956, what I was writing struck critics as the most old-fashioned rubbish—a sort of throw-back to the romanticism of Yeats—or even earlier, of Shelley and Blake. The success of *The Outsider* was followed by an almost immediate back-swing. The father figure of English logical positivism, A. J. Ayer, led the attack, in a review of *The Outsider,* while Arthur Koestler dismissed the book as 'bubble of the year' (and has since reprinted this opinion in a volume of essays, by way of reaffirming it). The word 'woolly' turned up increasingly in reviews, particularly of *Religion and the Rebel,* the sequel to *The Outsider.* Then there was another group of objectors on political grounds. Most of my contemporaries in literature were left-wing—Osborne, Amis, Braine, Doris Lessing, Christopher Logue, Kenneth Tynan, Wesker *et al.,* and they advocated the importance of 'commitment,' marching to Aldermaston, signing petitions against repressive regimes, and so on. I had no positive objections; I would have been entirely in favour of banning the H bomb or allowing Russia's Jews to go to Israel. It was just a question of priorities. I was interested in my own inner needs, and in the inner needs of men in general. That was my concept of an Outsider: a man driven by a powerful inner compulsion to freedom, which might lead him to act in opposition to the demands of society, to his own desire for comfort and acceptance by his fellows. In the nineteenth century, it had driven many of the major artists to an early grave; and most of the romantics accepted this as part of their basic philosophy: if you experience this strange urge for 'dim hills and far horizons,' expect an early death; this busy human world has no place for you. I wrote *The Outsider* because I couldn't accept this notion. I could see no *a priori* reason why Shelley and Keats had to die young, why Hölderlin and Nietzsche had to go insane, why Beddoes and Van Gogh had to commit suicide. Or, for that matter, why Wordsworth and Swinburne had to drift into a mediocre old age. To me, it seemed, quite simply, that most of them were *too passive*. Even Nietzsche, that advocate of war and ruthlessness, spent his life quietly drifting from *pension* to *pension*. I believed that if 'the Outsider' could learn to know himself, and make a determined effort to control his life instead of drifting, he might end as a leader of civilisation instead of one of its rejects. But the answer was *not* to join the peace corps or march in protest rallies. And because I held this indifferent attitude to current politics, I found myself, to my astonishment, labelled a fascist. I didn't see the logic of this, and still don't. I assume they thought that Individualism always leads to fascism—unaware that fascism is a form of socialism that exalts the state above the individual. At all events, I had to get used to a feeling of working alone that was rather like being sent to Coventry. I continued to write books. The success of *The Outsider* meant that I was able to find publishers. But reviews were dismissive, and in a few cases (such as *Introduction to the New Existentialism*) there were no reviews at all.

Lack of money made life difficult; but otherwise, I didn't mind too much. After all, I was arguing that the romantic Outsiders had been destroyed because they lacked the strength to stand alone. To allow myself to be depressed by the neglect would have been illogical. Anyway, I was too busy just keeping alive. So I completely failed to notice that something strange was happening. The tide of a century and a half was turning. I knew, of course, that there was an increasingly strong movement towards anti-reductionism in science. Since 1959 I had been in correspondence with the American psychologist Abraham Maslow, who believed that Freud had 'sold human nature short,' and that the idealistic and creative part of man's nature is as fundamental as his sexual or aggressive drives. I knew Michael Polanyi's important book *Personal Knowledge* (1958), arguing that the scientist's creative processes are as inspirational and illogical as the poet's, and that this is true of all creative thinking. But it came as a surprise to me to learn that there was suddenly a new wave of interest in eastern philosophy, in romanticism, in magic and occultism. When I wrote about the novels of Hermann Hesse in *The Outsider,* they were all out of print; and, as far as I know, I was the first person to write about them extensively in English. Now, suddenly, he was apparently a best-seller. So was Tolkien; his *Lord of the Rings* had been a 'cult book' since its publication in the mid-fifties, read and re-read by a small circle of enthusiasts; now it literally sold by the million in paperback on American campuses. So did H. P. Lovecraft, a writer I had first read in the early sixties, and had written about in a book called *The Strength to Dream* in 1962. When I first wrote about him, his books could only be obtained through a tiny American publisher, Arkham House, run by Lovecraft's old friend, August Derleth; by the late sixties, they were all in paperback.

As to the 'occult boom,' it seems to have started with a curious work called *The Morning of the Magicians,* by Louis Pauwels and Jacques Bergier, published in Paris in 1960. This also became a best-seller. And this in itself was a baffling phenomenon. There had always been offbeat best-sellers, like *The Search for Bridey Murphy, Worlds in Collision, The Passover Plot* (suggesting that the Resurrection was basically a put-up job); but they confined themselves to one particular theory. *The Morning of the Magicians* (translated in

English as *The Dawn of Magic*) had no central thesis. It moves from Gurdjieff to alchemy to the Great Pyramid to Atlantis to the question of whether Hitler was mixed up in black magic, and there are sections on Lovecraft, Arthur Machen and Charles Fort. The English edition is a few pages longer than the American; the pages that have been cut out of the U.S. edition describe an experiment in telepathy conducted between the atomic submarine *Nautilus* and the Westinghouse Special Research Center; presumably they were dropped because it was impossible to obtain the necessary confirmation from Westinghouse or the U.S. Navy. Which raises the question of how many other items in the book might be equally difficult to confirm. . . . A fascinating book, certainly, but one that would enrage any logical positivist because its authors seem to have an attitude of blissful indifference towards questions of proof and verification. Although the English and American editions have had nothing like the success of the French, they certainly played an important part in the 'occult revival' that now proceeded to snowball. Small presses that had specialised in occult books for a limited audience suddenly found they were making unprecedented sums of money. Copies of works like John Symonds's biography of Aleister Crowley, *The Great Beast*—first published in 1951 by Rider, England's foremost 'occult press'—and Israel Regardie's four-volume work on the rituals of the Golden Dawn, changed hands at fantastic prices. Witch covens sprang up all over the place—until 1951 they had been illegal in England—encouraged by a book called *Witchcraft Today* by Gerald Gardner, in which it was claimed that witchcraft—the ancient pagan nature religion of 'Wicca'—still flourished more widely than anyone had supposed. Whether it really did, or whether it was Gardner's book that caused it to flourish, is perhaps beside the point. In the late sixties, a seven-volume encyclopedia of occultism, *Man, Myth and Magic,* published in weekly parts, achieved the kind of success that had previously been achieved only by cookery books and works like Wells's *Outline of History.* The works of every neglected Kabbalist, from Paracelsus to Crowley, began to find their way back into print.

Now Wells would have said that the 'occult boom' indicates nothing except that people are stupid and gullible, and there is obviously some truth in this view. But I believe it is far more than that. It is all part of what might be called 'the new romanticism.' The 'old romanticism' dates back just about two centuries before the occult revival; it may be said to have started with Rousseau's *Nouvelle Héloïse* in 1760; and Rousseau's book is basically a plea for freedom: that a man and woman who are in love have a right to become lovers without the approval of society. And all romanticism has continued to be an obsession with freedom: the feeling that freedom can be found if you go and look for it. It runs from Byron's *Childe Harold* to Hesse's *Siddartha* and Jack Kerouac's *On the Road.* The interesting thing about this new incarnation of the spirit of romanticism is that it came so late. The old romanticism may be said to have died out in the last decade of the nineteenth century, the *fin de siècle;* its last avatars were Rimbaud, Verlaine, Dowson, Lionel Johnson, and those other poets of what Yeats called 'the tragic generation.' After that, there was a reaction: back to realism, classicism, social responsibility. From the twilight sadness of Verlaine and Dowson, there was a plunge into the savage pessimism of the 1920s—Eliot, Pound, Hemingway, Huxley, Joyce. The writers of the thirties rallied, pulling themselves back from the brink; they wrote about dole queues, the war in Spain, social responsibility. Then came the war; and after it, a sense of hiatus. Nobody seemed to know where to go next. The American sociologist David Riesman wrote an essay called 'The Found Generation' about the new generation of students; it seemed that they were no longer full of political idealism, like Riesman's generation of the thirties; all they wanted was a good job, a suburban house and a car.

When I wrote *The Outsider* in 1955, it seemed to me that I was swimming in direct opposition to the current of the times. Nobody was interested in Nietzsche and Hesse and Nijinsky. Yet Kerouac's *On the Road* had, in fact, been written three years earlier and when it finally appeared, in 1957, it was clear that America also had its generation of dissatisfied romantics who thought that freedom lay just around the corner—in San Francisco, or New Mexico, or perhaps in Death Valley, where Charles Manson's 'family' were arrested in 1969. Within ten years, the new romanticism had transformed the face of society in Europe and America; the students were marching and protesting again, and the 'Beatniks' (the name was coined by a San Francisco columnist) outnumbered holidaymakers in seaside resorts. Psychedelic drugs and marijuana also played their part in the revolution. In 1953, Aldous Huxley's book *The Doors of Perception* had advocated the use of mescalin to produce 'expanded consciousness,' but it was another ten years before mescalin and LSD became as common as marijuana. An Englishman who settled in America, Alan Watts, became the prophet of this new generation of 'mescalin eaters'; his doctrine asserts basically that western man has become too aggressive towards nature; he must learn to stop 'running,' to become passive and receptive. Dr. John Lilly's important book *The Centre of the Cyclone* also advocates the controlled use of psychedelic drugs for 'inner exploration,' and goes into considerable detail about the techniques for this 'journey to the interior.' Carlos Castaneda's three books about his 'magical apprenticeship' to the Yacqui Indian medicine-man, don Juan, have all achieved the status of best-sellers; but, on close examination, it is difficult to see why. Walter Goldschmidt, who introduces the first (*The Teachings of Don Juan*), begins by admitting that it is partly allegory, and Castaneda's accounts of his meeting with the *peyotl* god Mescalito, and of his flight through the air when he rubs himself with a special ointment, sound like exercises in imaginative fiction. Castaneda's books are best-sellers because they express the aspirations of the new romanticism so clearly: the desire to escape to 'other worlds,' the suggestion that drugs are a valid means to this end, the serious tone of the discussions about expanded consciousness. But unlike the popular classics of the old romanticism—Goethe's *Werther,* Schiller's *Robbers*—the don Juan books make a claim to be fact, not fiction; and this is most important of all. As 'imaginary conversations with don Juan,' their appeal would have been much smaller. The desire to escape has become more serious, more urgent, than it was in the nineteenth century; it hungers for fact.

The association between Hippie culture and occultism can be seen at Glastonbury, a town whose small population (just over four thousand) is almost outnumbered by the influx of Hippies during the summer months. The man largely responsible for this is a shy, rather aloof scholar named John Michell. Michell's book *The View Over Atlantis* appeared in 1969; in it, he discusses the theories of Alfred Watkins, a Hereford businessman, first expounded in *The Old Straight Track* (1925). Watkins had noticed many straight tracks associated with prehistoric mounds (or tumps), marked at intervals with large stones; he assumed that these were the roads of prehistoric man. John Michell's first book had dealt with 'flying saucers,' and he observed that UFOs are often associated with spots where leys intersect—like Cradle Hill, at Warminster. In *The View Over Atlantis,* he suggests that these leys were 'lines of power' analogous to the Chinese 'dragon paths,' lines associated with the power called *fung-shui,* the ancient energies of the earth. Certain leys link up St. Michael's Mount in Cornwall with Glastonbury Tor and Stonehenge; all Britain is intersected with these paths, which were associated with some ancient civilisation that was of a far higher order than anyone has so far guessed. (This is his 'Atlantis.') In a subsequent book, *City of Revelation,* Michell expands this theory that the Golden Age is more than a legend; that it really existed at some remote epoch, and that information about it is concealed, in coded form, in many ancient buildings, including Stonehenge. Two central conclusions emerge from all this. One is that, during this remote epoch, man was in spiritual harmony with nature, in the way that native magicians and *shamans* (like don Juan) still are; the other, that man owed his knowledge, in this remote epoch, to extraterrestrial beings. (This is an idea that seems to be in the air of our time; Arthur C. Clarke gave it popular currency in his film script for *2001, A Space Odyssey,* in which beings from outer space land on earth, and leave behind a monolith whose vibrations have the effect of heightening the intelligence of man's remote ancestors.)

In the fifties, Michell's books would have been classified with 'the lunatic fringe' (as Watkins's book was), and would have reached the tiny audience who study the measurements of the Great Pyramid and the mediaeval cathedrals. It is an interesting sign of our time that they should have inspired the Hippie invasion of Glastonbury. It seems unlikely that his basic ideas can have wide appeal; the form in which he presents them is too abstruse, often mathematical. But what certainly *does* appeal is this romantic idea of lines of power connecting spots like Stonehenge, Woodhenge, Salisbury Cathedral, Maiden Castle, and so on. The imaginative appeal of Michell's work is related to that of Lovecraft and Tolkien; but again, like Castaneda, he has the advantage of presenting his work as fact, or at least, serious speculation.

The occult boom shows no sign of letting up. If history runs true to form, it should continue until about the turn of the century. For there have been magical revivals in almost every century for the past five hundred years. Towards the end of the sixteenth century, there was John Dee and a host of other practising magicians and alchemists. It skipped a century—the intellectual atmosphere of the age of Newton, Leibniz and Descartes was not conducive to magic—but the late eighteenth century was the age of Mesmer, St. Germain, Cagliostro, and the late nineteenth century was the age of Madame Blavatsky, Eliphas Lévi, the Golden Dawn. In terms of the number of people actually affected, the latest revival is the greatest of all. For example, it is a curious fact that the best-selling author in the whole world at the moment is Erich von Däniken, a German whose *Chariots of the Gods?—Unsolved Mysteries of the Past,* appeared in 1969 and became a best-seller; since then, *Return to the Stars* and *Gold of the Gods* have broken all records. I say it is a curious fact because von Däniken's books say nothing that has not already been said many times by various writers. His basic thesis is the one we have already mentioned: that in some remote age, 'gods' from flying saucers landed on the earth, and helped create a highly evolved civilisation, whose ruins can still be seen

in the jungles of South America, on Easter Island, etc.
His theses are fascinating, if not new; but the manner
in which he states them is, to put it mildly, highly unsatisfactory. He gives the impression of being unable to
stick to a point, rambling wildly so that it is difficult to
follow the argument. There is an element of boastfulness
which unsympathetic critics have interpreted as para-
noia. (*Chariots of the Gods?* begins, typically: 'It took
courage to write this book, and it will take courage to
read it,' both statements being patently untrue.) The
style is often infantile, full of jibes and jeers at his critics;
speaking of a gold hemisphere with a circular brim: 'To
anticipate fatuous objections, it is not a sculptural repre-
sentation of a hat with a brim. Hats have hollow spaces
for even the most stupid heads to fit into.' And in places,
he displays a lack of logic that amounts almost to imbe-
cility. Describing a skeleton carved out of stone which
he located in an underground chamber, he says: 'I
counted ten pairs of ribs, all anatomically accurate. Were
there anatomists who dissected bodies for the prehistoric
sculptor? As we know, Wilhelm Conrad Röntgen did not
discover the new kind of rays he called X-rays until
1895!' The mind boggles at the mad illogicality: the idea
that a sculptor would need X-rays to see a skeleton,
when every graveyard must have been full of them. It
is equally puzzling how his publishers allowed him to
put such an absurdity into print.

At the beginning of *Gold of the Gods,* he claims to
have investigated a system of underground tunnels in
South America, 'thousands of miles in length,' containing the ruins of the ancient civilisation for which the
astronaut 'gods' were responsible. He even offers a map
of the area in which the 'secret entrance' is located, but
since the area covered by the map is a few thousand
square miles, it cannot be regarded as conclusive evi-

dence of his good faith. Obviously, if von Däniken leads investigators to his tunnel system, he will achieve a celebrity that will outshine that of his best-selling books, and will confound all his critics. But at the moment, it must be admitted that the chaotic nature of his books *does* support the view that he is a charlatan and a crank.

But again I must emphasise: it is the *presentation* of the books that suggests this, not their subject matter. Ever since UFO sightings began, soon after the Second World War, many people have pointed out that ancient texts—including the Bible—refer to objects that sound like UFOs, that ancient drawings and carvings often show disc-like objects that could be flying saucers, and odd-looking men who could be astronauts in flying kit. It is an unproved hypothesis; but to give it serious consideration is not necessarily the sign of a crank.

I was asked if I would care to write a book on the occult in 1968. It sounded an amusing idea. Ever since those early days in London, I had been interested in the subject, although I tended to treat it as light reading. When I was in America, on a lecture tour, in 1961, I bought paperbacks about flying saucers and allied topics at every airport bookstall, and I also purchased most of the books on occult topics issued by University Books in New York: Montague Summers on witches, werewolves and vampires, reprints of the books of A. E. Waite on the Rosicrucians, the Kabbalah, and so on. Moreover, since an experience with mescalin in 1963, *I had* developed my own theory of man's 'unused powers.' I had disliked the mescalin experience. There were none of the usual visual effects; everything looked much as usual; it was rather like being drunk, but with less control. For some odd reason, I had a strong intuition that the district in which I live—in south Cornwall—was once associated with witchcraft. I have never tried to verify this; my wife can find nothing about it in books of local history. What interested me was that my mind seemed more intuitive, more telepathic, as it were. I recalled that Jim Corbett, the famous tiger hunter, said that after years of hunting man eaters, he had developed a sort of sixth sense about danger, which he called 'jungle sensitivity.' I could understand this. The mind has sensitive areas, rather like the nerves in a fish's sides, that register delicate pressures. Most animals seem to possess this 'sixth sense'—in *The Occult* I cited many cases; of the homing instinct in birds and animals, of 'foreknowledge' in dogs—for example, how Hugh McDiarmid's dog knows when he is going to return home from a long journey, and sits at the end of the lane a couple of days before he is due back, waiting. Man must also have possessed this same 'psychic sensitivity' in the distant past. But he doesn't need it in modern civilised life; in fact, it would be a nuisance. My mescalin experience may have made me more sensitive, more intuitive; but it also ruined my normal powers of concentration. In order to tackle the complex business of civilised living, we must *narrow* our powers, concentrate on what has to be done. Intense will-drive and this telepathic intuition are incompatible. Neither would it be accurate to say that city life destroys the sixth sense; *we* destroy it in ourselves.

However, that is not the end of the matter. These powers have only gone into cold storage; they can be brought out again if needed—for example, if, like Jim Corbett, we return to circumstances where they become necessary for survival. But there is another possibility. They may return as a kind of by-product of another kind of power, a power that man is only now slowly learning to develop. A dog may be able to sense ghosts in an empty house. But no animal could experience the kind of excitement Heinrich Schliemann felt as he uncovered the walls of ancient Troy, or Howard Carter as he entered the chamber containing the coffin of Tutankhamen. This excitement is based on what we might call 'a direct sense of otherness,' of other times and other places. It could be objected that this sense of otherness is 'nothing but imagination,' but a moment's thought will show that this is careless thinking. It is true that Schliemann could not really look into the past, to the Troy of eleven centuries B.C. But the words 'Homer's Troy,' which, for most of us, are merely words, suddenly became a reality for Schliemann. Troy *was* a reality, and for a moment, Schliemann was able to grasp it as such, as if he had been transported back three thousand years.

This is a point of vital importance. The mind possesses a power to focus reality. Everyone has experienced this on the first day of a holiday, when everything seems clearer and fresher than usual. In the mood of holiday excitement, we seem to see things in sharper focus, and we also experience a stronger sense of the reality of other times; if I happen to read something about Michelangelo or Beethoven in this mood, they no longer seem remote figures of history; I can grasp that they were real men, like myself. This power to 'focus reality' is the ability to project a *beam of interest*. All creatures have this ability—you have only to see the way a dog hangs around the house of a bitch in heat to see that dogs can be as single-minded as humans—but animals can only direct it at the present moment. When you take your dog for a country walk, you can watch his beam of interest switching from object to object—a rabbit hole, a gap in the hedge, an old bone. If an aeroplane goes overhead, he does not look up into the sky; that is too remote. And if you meet a friend on your walk, and stop to have a leisurely conversation about a neighbour who died ten years ago, your mind has gone into a realm where your dog cannot follow you; you have, casually and without effort, directed your beam of interest to another time and another place.

Human beings can not only direct their beam of interest to distant realities; they can direct it to realities that never existed. A novel like Wells's *Time Machine* or David Lindsay's *Voyage to Arcturus* demonstrates this extraordnary power of the human mind to evoke a non-existent reality as vividly as if the novel were a volume of travels in Central Africa. And a man like H. P. Lovecraft, bored and dissatisfied with his life in Providence, Rhode Island, can create a fictional 'reality' that reveals that he has trained his mind to focus on a self-created mental world. What is interesting here is that Lovecraft led a rather unsatisfying, unfulfilled existence; it would have been understandable if, like an undernourished child, he had drifted aimlessly and died without having achieved anything. In fact, he learned to *generate* some of the 'psychological vitamins' he needed by an act of imagination; in spite of a thoroughly frustrating life, he managed to grow into a remarkable human being. This is as startling as if a half starved man put on weight by imagining five-course meals. Man's power to direct his 'beam of interest' at distant realities obviously has some fascinating implications; it gives him a new kind of power over his own life.

This power is not yet highly developed in human beings. I have called it 'Faculty X'; for it is, in effect, a new faculty, the faculty that distinguishes man from all other animals: the faculty that may be considered the real aim of human evolution.

But this Faculty X is not an *alternative* to the animal's intuitive powers. Man discarded his sixth sense because he couldn't afford to keep it; civilisation used up all his surplus energies, and he had none left over to operate a sixth sense. But Faculty X represents a new level of power over himself; psychic energies are freed: it could be compared to the flood of manpower that occurs at the end of a war, when the army is demobilised. Once again he can afford to develop his 'psychic radar,' his sixth sense. This is why I believe that, as man develops Faculty X, his so-called psychic powers will also increase— second sight, telepathy, the ability to dowse, even astral projection.

Why do I think so? My own psychic powers are certainly unremarkable. My temperament is basically scientific. Like Wells, I experienced a tremendous sense of imaginative release through the vision of science; at the age of eleven, the atomic table of the elements struck me as more poetic than anything written by Shakespeare. And although I abandoned science for literature at the age of sixteen or so, the temperament remains; it is ideas and facts that excite me, and the process of fitting them into larger and larger patterns. Such a temperament is not likely to be very 'psychic.' I cannot dowse; I have never seen a ghost; I have never had any experience of foreknowledge or pre-vision; and my few unimportant telepathic experiences are summarised in a couple of pages of *The Occult*. But I still note that a kind of 'jungle sensitiveness' appears when I am healthy and 'on top of things.'

I can give an example of this. One morning every week, I drive into Mevagissey, a couple of miles away, to buy groceries and pick up our cleaning lady. One morning a few months ago—the exact date was 8 January 1973—I was meditating as I drove in: by which I mean that I was thinking seriously, trying to deepen an insight, to do with the way we respond to crisis. The answer came to me, accompanied by a sense of control and relaxation. The narrow lane that leads up to our house makes an acute angle with an almost equally narrow country road, and getting around this corner, without having to stop and reverse, is a matter of some skill. As I was about to swing into the drive, the thought entered my head: 'Wait. The post van may be coming out.' I had no reason to think so, for in more than ten years living in this house, I haven't met the post van in the lane more than twice. But I went into first gear, and took the corner very cautiously—and the post van pulled up within a few inches of my bonnet. Two weeks ago, the same thing happened again; before I made the difficult turn into the drive, I had a faint, nagging discomfort, like a very distant bell—and once again, met the post van. I am not saying there might have been a violent head-on collision if I hadn't had this 'warning' feeling; but some psychic radar knew the post van was there, and was taking no chances. In both cases, I was feeling wide-awake, psychologically healthy, not anxious or passive.

Having said which, I have defined the underlying theme that I wish to explore in this book. Writers on the 'supernatural' have often noted that some mediums seem to be sturdy, healthy people, not at all like the usual image of the 'sensitive.' Not many months ago, I watched Harry Edwards give one of his final demonstrations of 'spirit healing' before his retirement (at the age of eighty), and afterwards had the pleasure of a conversation with him, which he allowed me to tape. I was struck by his utter normality and 'factualness'; he looked, and sounded, more like a healthy farmer than a spirit healer. I was startled when I read, a few weeks later, that he was nearly eighty; I would have placed his age at sixty-five. Everything about him seemed to confirm my theory that 'psychic powers' are a natural consequence of psychological health.

Since writing *The Occult,* I have met three people who seem to confirm my supposition that unusual powers may be a kind of by-product of complete 'normality'; and since all three seem to me to deserve more space than I could reasonably offer them in my second projected volume of *The Occult,* I have decided to devote this short book to them; it should be regarded as a postscript to the first volume.

I have one intense regret. In *The Occult* I quoted *Witches,* by T. C. Lethbridge, on the subject of dowsing. Subsequently, I became aware of his other three books, *Gogmagog, Ghost and Ghoul* and *Ghost and Divining-Rod,* and I realised that Lethbridge is a very important figure indeed. A man with a thoroughly scientific turn of mind, he takes dowsing as his starting point, and goes on to develop a convincing theory of ghosts and what he calls ghouls—unpleasant feelings experienced at spots where some tragedy has taken place. I sent him a copy of *The Occult* together with a letter asking him if I could come and see him; his wife replied to say that he had died the previous autumn (1971). As a tribut to a remarkable man, I dedicate this book to his memory.

CHAPTER ONE

ROBERT LEFTWICH

It was sometime in the first half of 1971 that the encyclopedia *Man, Myth and Magic*—which was being published in weekly parts—appeared with a back cover headed: 'Psychic Sales Manager.' Robert Leftwich, said the unsigned article, began to develop his psychic powers while still at school, and since adulthood, his range of psychic experiences has greatly widened. The article began: 'Robert Leftwich is a man of apparently limitless physical and mental energy. He literally bounds from place to place and from subject to subject with a vigour which is little short of astonishing.' His interests and accomplishments were then listed: ' . . . he is sales manager of a large firm of pumping and hydraulic engineers [and] also an enthusiastic philosopher, writer, antiquarian book specialist, dowser, archaeologist and occultist. In the latter field, he has located and exorcised a ghost in his own home,* developed powers of thought

* The ghost was a presence, associate with a 'cold spot,' in the sitting room. Leftwich walked into this cold spot one night and asked the 'presence' if it could hear him. 'If you can hear me, I want you to move the picture from over the mantelpiece to the other side of the room.' Nothing happened. But in the night, there was a noise, and the next morning, the picture had been thrown across the room. The ghost never made itself felt again.

transference and partial recognition, successfully experimented with most branches of extra-sensory perception, and projected his "astral body" consciously over distances.' It quoted him as saying that he did not consider himself unique: 'Anyone can develop his latent mental powers if he tries hard enough.'

It was this that interested me so much. Leftwich sounded like a walking illustration of the ideas I had developed in *The Occult*.

By this, I do not mean I considered him an example of 'Faculty X.' This is a point I had better clear up immediately. Faculty X could be defined as a highly developed power to envisage the reality of other times and places. In *The Occult* I cited a number of cases: for example, Arnold Toynbee's sudden feeling, as he sat among the ruins of the citadel of Mistra, that the intervening years had become unreal, and that the barbarians who destroyed Mistra might suddenly pour over that horizon. . . .

Such an experience is not the prerogative of poets and historians. In 1960, I interviewed a lady who lived at 29 Hanbury Street, the site of Jack the Ripper's murder of Annie Chapman in 1888. She told me an amusing anecdote of a young woman who visited the house, and asked to go to the lavatory; her hostess escorted her to the lavatory in the back yard, and stood waiting. She said: 'From where you're sitting, you can see the exact spot where Jack the Ripper cut open that woman.' The girl shrieked, jumped off the lavatory, and rushed clumsily across the yard—somewhat incapacitated by the knickers that were still around her ankles. Now, she *knew* the murder had taken place in the previous century, so it was not sudden fear that the Ripper might revisit the scene that made her scream. It was a sudden imaginative vision of a murder that wiped out the intervening years, the realisation that she was looking at the spot that had been seen by the Ripper and his victim.

But this flash of Faculty X had to be stimulated by a particular set of circumstances—a rather sinister slum yard on a winter evening. . . . Places are great stimulators of Faculty X. It is rarer to be able to achieve the same 'free vision' through reading or study—although all lovers of poetry know the experience of gradually raising themselves into a curious state of freedom through the reading of favourite poems. This demands what Keats called 'negative capability,' the power to lose all sense of one's own personality, to 'open up' and become a little more than a sensitive receptor.

The reason this is so rare becomes clear if one accepts the concept of the 'hierarchy of needs' or values, developed by the psychologist Abraham Maslow.* Maslow suggested that our sense of values develops in a certain order. A man who is starving can conceive of nothing more desirable than a good meal every day. If he achieves this, he begins to think about security, a roof over his head. If he achieves this, he begins to think about sex, love, marriage, children. And if the sexual needs are securely satisfied, the next level of need to emerge is self-steem, the desire to be liked, respected. (This is the stage at which men join rotary clubs and women hold coffee mornings.) Finally, there is the creative level: the need to do a job well for the pleasure of it. It need not be artistic creation; it might be collecting stamps or landscape gardening. A woman who is good at bringing up children might adopt children when her own are grown up, and Maslow would regard this as an expression of creativity rather than sexual (maternal) instinct. Now obviously, the true development

* For a fuller account, see my *New Pathways in Psychology*, Gollancz 1972.

of Faculty X requires a negative capability, an absorption in 'other realities' for their own sake, which is unlikely to appear at any level of the hierarchy except this creative level. On other levels, it may appear as an accidental flash; but it is not likely to be cultivated. (And note that the self-esteem level already possesses a considerable degree of impersonal absorption—or can possess it; for example, a rotarian might derive equal pleasure from the respect of his fellow rotarians, and from the social good that he does by his efforts.) So psychic powers, even in a highly disciplined person, do not necessarily imply Faculty X.

All the same, Leftwich's conviction that anyone can develop psychic powers appealed to me as an important step in the direction of Faculty X. And the descriptions of his own powers, as outlined in the article, were certainly fascinating. At school, Leftwich told his interviewer, he discovered how to avoid memorising the whole of long prose extracts or poems. He would memorise a particular passage; then, when the master went round the class, picking out boys at random to recite passages, Leftwich would will him to select *him* for the passage he'd learned. As an adult, he had 'more or less willed himself into his present job.' Other powers he had developed included dowsing, astral projection, and the dispersal of clouds by an act of will. He tells an anecdote of astral projection: 'The wife of a friend of mine was scoffing at the subject one evening, and I suggested that she devise a test for me. She told me that she had a mole on a certain part of her body. If I could tell her where it was, she would be more favourably disposed to my arguments. The following evening, I relaxed and quite easily left the body and willed myself into her home some miles away. She was in her bathroom, preparing to get into the bath, and I had no difficulty in spotting the mole—she was extremely alarmed when I told her the following day.' He added that while watching her 'astrally,' he felt no sexual urge.

The article went on to speak of his dowsing ability, and ended with a note on his convictions. His religious leanings are towards Buddhism. 'Despite his comfortable surroundings, his personal life is almost as austere as that of a Buddhist monk. He is a strict vegetarian, a teetotaler, a non-smoker, and even abstains from tea and coffee, explaining that any form of stimulant is capable of interfering with his powers. He also says that sexual excess can disrupt the mind and cause the mental processes to function inefficiently—and that for this reason sexual activities are best limited to occasions when conception is desired.'

I decided I ought to try and contact Leftwich. Although *The Occult* had contained a number of accounts of 'psychic' experiences by various friends—A. L. Rowse, Robert Graves, Louis Singer, Ronald Duncan—I had never actually met anyone who claimed to have positive psychic abilities, i.e. the power to *make* things happen, rather than simply experience them. Fortunately, Leftwich's address was mentioned in the article —which mentioned that his house is the highest house in Sussex. So I wrote to him, asking him about this power to disperse clouds,* and whether he could give me a few more details about the techniques for develop-

---

* A well authenticated experiment in cloud dispersal took place at Orillia, in Canada, witnessed by press and television. This experiment—which was successful—is described in *Power of the Mind* by Rolf Alexander, and a photograph of the demonstration is included in the book. In June 1956, the Associated Rediffusion programme 'This Week' showed a film of a similar successful demonstration on Hampstead Heath, and the 30 June issue of *Picture Post* contains an article by Fyfe Robertson on the same subject, with photographs by Alex Dellow. I wish to thank Mr. D. Phillips of Dundee for pointing this out to me.

ing it. An answer came back fairly promptly—apparently he had read my book, and was interested in the suggestion that I might put him into the sequel. He said that the dispersal of clouds was extremely difficult, but that it was quite easy to demonstrate psychokinesis, the mind's power to directly influence matter. In the envelope, he included a small square of paper, which had been folded from corner to corner, and also across the middle—giving an effect like a Union Jack with a St. George's Cross and St. Andrew's Cross. He told me to fold this in the form of a paper dart with four fins, balance it on a needle stuck in a cork, and try willing it to go round. He mentioned that it was best to tie a handkerchief over the nose and mouth, so as not to breathe on it.

I decided to try it. I folded the paper into a dart, stuck a needle on a cork, and put the paper dart on top of it, so it looked like a fairground roundabout. Then I tied a handkerchief round my face, cupped my hands round the dart, and concentrated on it, trying to push the dart with my gaze, as it were. I concentrated till I was red in the face, but it didn't budge. My face began to get hot and sticky under the handkerchief. I decided to put the roundabout on my work bench, which is waist high, so I could crouch below the level of the bench and breathe normally. That didn't work either. I put it back on my desk, beside my typewriter, and went on with my writing, periodically looking up quickly to try to catch it off guard. It was all no good.

It was the next day, I believe, that I tried again. Having wasted so much effort earlier, I now no longer tried to do it by sheer willpower. Instead, I tried to persuade it to move, so to speak. To my surprise, it began to do so. It was a warm day, with the sun streaming in the window, and it struck me that perhaps the heat from the palms of my hands was causing warm air to rise; I moved them back further, so the fingertips were only just touching. Using 'imagination' rather than sheer force, I got it to stop and move in the opposite direction. My wife came down to bring me a cup of tea, and I demonstrated it to her. I no longer bothered about the handkerchief over my face, being certain that the 'roundabout' was far enough away from my face not to be affected; anyway, my breath was going downwards, below the edge of my desk, a foot away. As amazing as it seemed, it actually worked. I left it on my table, and practised periodically later in the day, sometimes not even cupping my hands around it. When I told Leftwich about it in a letter, he replied that the element of *imagining* it moving was crucial.

Some weeks later—in July 1971—I had to drive to Hastings, then to London. Crowborough lay on my route, so I asked Leftwich if it would be convenient to call on him. He said it would. So, on a very hot Monday morning, I set out for Crowborough. I wasn't sure what kind of a person I was going to meet: whether he would prove to be alarming, or impressive, or perhaps just a fraud. Somehow, I pictured him as a rather quiet, pipe-smoking man—although I knew he didn't smoke.

I expected the highest house in Sussex to stand alone on a remote hilltop outside the town; in fact, it proved to be one of a row of houses on a tree-lined road. It was smaller than I'd expected, but very pretty, and obviously very old, built of grey stone. The lawns were large and smooth. It was only about three in the afternoon, but I knew he'd be home—I'd rung him the night before. He heard the car, which I parked beside his own, and came out to meet me. A very rapid, firm handshake, and 'Nice to see you. Come on in.' I realised that the photographs in *Man, Myth and Magic* had bestowed a false air of repose on him. He had a way of talking and moving rapidly, although without any suggestion of nervous tension. We went through the back garden and into the house. His sitting room had an air of polished neatness. My own house, while not chaotic, is never exactly tidy; the floor is usually covered with books, toys and children's records, and if you move the armchair you are likely to knock over a wine bottle that has been there since the night before. Robert Leftwich's beautifully tidy room made me feel a little uncomfortable.

I said I hoped he hadn't come home early especially for me. He said No, he usually managed to do a full day's work in half a day; and since his job involved driving around and making calls, no one was any the wiser if he came home early. He said most people wasted their energy; he always threw himself into whatever he did, and did it with maximum speed and efficiency.

I talked about my idea of putting him into a book. He said *he* had also written a book—and promptly produced me the typescript—and asked me whether there was money in writing. I said not much, and gave him a brief run-down on the money one is likely to make from a book. He didn't seem too downcast. 'How much do you think I make?' Looking out of the window at his enormous back garden, I made a guess: 'Ten thousand a year?' He chuckled and shook his head. 'Three thousand. And out of that, I usually manage to save twelve hundred a year.' 'What for?' 'I intend to retire when I'm fifty.' 'And what then?' 'I want to buy a caravan. Perhaps I shall go and live in France. I want to be able to spend the rest of my life developing myself, working out my ideas, writing books. . . .'

Somehow, it was difficult to talk to him about 'occultism'—although he had an excellent library of occult books. (He is listed in various trade publications as a dealer; this, apparently, was a sideline.) Not that he was evasive. He seemed to talk with complete frankness. He had a brisk, good-humoured air, and always seemed to be smiling. His conversation seemed to drag him along hectically from subject to subject. His accent was somewhat public-school, and public-school English has a slightly explosive sound, as if the words are being fired from a gun; Leftwich's nervous energy emphasised this, so his conversation was like a series of small detonations. He is obviously a highly sociable man, intensely interested in people—he mentioned getting into conversations on trains with strangers several times. If I'd met him casually, I wouldn't have dreamed that he was associated with any form of 'occultism.' He might have been a house master at Harrow. And his obsession with order and tidiness deepened this impression. He explained his daily routine: up at 6.30, shredded wheat for breakfast, a vegetarian lunch, no tea, his last meal at six, a glass of orange juice at nine, and off to bed by ten. . . . (I may have some of the details wrong, but that was the general impression.)

We talked about dowsing, and he explained that this was simply a kind of offshoot of this basic faculty to 'make things happen.' For example, he had me place a coin under the carpet, on a certain line, while he looked the other way. Then he took a dowsing rod—two curved staves attached together at one end—and walked across the room. The rod dipped violently as he came over the coin. He explained that I could place some other object under the carpet—for example, a letter—and that if he then 'dowsed' for that, his rod would ignore the coin and only dip when it came over the letter. He also demonstrated to me that he could make the rod dip for *everything but* the penny; he walked across the room with it twisting violently in his hands, until he

stood over the coin, when it became quiescent. I recalled
T. C. Lethbridge's remark that everyone possesses the
dowsing faculty potentially, but that in some people it
is so weak as to be unnoticeable; Lethbridge uses the
comparison of a portable radio, which will not play if
the battery is flat. The implication is that a man needs to
have a highly charged battery to be a good dowser. Leftwich certainly gave the impression of being highly
charged.

His children came home from school—both under
ten. We walked in the garden, and he remarked, with
characteristic frankness, that he doesn't feel he is cut
out to be a husband and father; he is fond of his children, but doesn't feel he has any vocation in that direction. This 'figured,' as the Americans say. The really
philoprogenitive parent has a strong 'negative capability';
Leftwich obviously finds the world too interesting to be
negative. In a way, he made me think of a young dog on
a country walk, intensely curious about everything, rush-
ing backwards and forwards. He certainly didn't look or
behave like a man close on fifty.

Altogether, I found him a paradoxical character, full
of apparent contradictions. The sexual asceticism is obviously genuine—the Tolstoyan view that sex is intended
for reproductory purposes, not as a plaything. On the
other hand, he always has been, and continues to be,
strongly interested in women; he seems to find them
more stimulating than men. His conversation is full of
flashes of intuitive insight into the workings of the mind,
the function of religion, human potentiality; yet in another way, his ideas seemed to be oddly materialistic,
sceptical. In the manuscript he presented me with, there
is a section on 'The Cause of Human Action,' and he
analyses religious feeling in a thoroughly simplistic, 're-
ductionist' manner. 'Many readers will insist that reli-

gious folk usually possess the quality of kindness as a natural basic attribute, but profound thought combined with absolute sincerity usually reveals the true cause for the supposed goodness. They undoubtedly appear most kind to onlookers, but their motives . . . (frequently unknown to themselves) are fundamentally of a selfish nature.' He goes on to mention a man who helped an old lady repair her radio set; when pressed, the man admitted that he enjoyed creating a favourable impression, and also enjoyed showing off his (limited) electrical knowledge to someone who would be impressed by it.

One senses immediately a certain lack of logic here, even if it is difficult to pin down. What were the man's motives *supposed* to have been—to entitle him to a clean moral bill of health? The old lady's son might have repaired her radio out of love of his mother; a kindly neighbour might have done it out of pity. Robert Leftwich's friend apparently admitted that helping her aided his inferiority complex. But unless he went into the house to steal her savings, it hardly matters why he did it. Under the pleasure in creating a favourable impression there was obviously the sense of responsibility for a fellow creature, which is what is at issue. But even if he had repaired the radio wholly out of some neurotic compulsion, this *still* would not prove that there is no such thing as a disinterested feeling of responsibility *for other people*. What *is* interesting is why Robert Leftwich should want to insist that most people do 'disinterested' acts out of 'selfish' motives. The answer is fairly clear, and I do not think it is particularly discreditable to him. He is deeply and intensely interested in himself, and there is no reason why he shouldn't be: he is an interesting man, bursting with ideas. He is also detached enough to feel a mild guilt about this. If all 'disinterested' conduct can be reduced to self-interest, there is no need to feel guilty. . . .

All of which is only to say that, in Maslow's terms, Leftwich still operates, to some extent, on the self-esteem level. In fact, with typical honesty, he admits this. He is one of Maslow's self-actualisers who has not yet actualised himself; this, he explained, was the reason that he wanted to retire at fifty and spend the rest of his life 'finding himself,' deepening his insights, exploring further depths of self-control.

When I left him, on that July afternoon, to drive to London, my feelings about him were ambivalent. I found him likeable, because of that child-like openness and frankness, and the enormous zest he puts into living. But I could imagine someone who didn't like him finding him an intolerable egoist; and this, in turn, would probably lead them to dismiss his 'powers' as wishful thinking. This, I was fairly certain, would be a mistake. His dowsing abilities are clearly extraordinary; he has even demonstrated them in front of a television audience. Obviously, he can 'do something' with his mind which enables him to tune in to things that are beyond the normal human radius. When he came to Cornwall, he demonstrated one of his abilities with both me and my wife. He stood with his back to us, holding the divining rod. One of us was told to walk forward until we crossed a spot where we knew there was an underground pipe. As we crossed the pipe, the rod in Robert's hand twisted to indicate water. He had 'tuned in' to our minds. At Beacon House, he had showed me photographs and business letters in connection with divining minerals *from an aeroplane,* and it was apparent that he had been successful. There could be no doubt that he possessed unusual powers. What I now wanted to understand was the nature of these powers, how he came to possess them, and their relation to his total personality.

At this point, I must temporarily leave Robert Leftwich, and speak more generally of the subject of dowsing.

In its simplest form, there is nothing 'supernatural' about dowsing—any more than there is about radio, or the way iron filings shape themselves along a magnet's field of force. Dowsing has been scientifically tested. (Descriptions of experiments can be found in Sir William Barrett's book *The Divining Rod* [1926].) In 1968, Robert Leftwich performed under controlled test conditions on a TV programme compèred by Brian Inglis, and located three cans of water that had been buried in a certain area of ground. Although he converted a sceptic—Professor John Cohen—Leftwich himself was disappointed; five cans of water and a knife had been buried, and he failed to locate all these.

T. C. Lethbridge asserts (in *Ghost and Divining-Rod*) that all objects have a field of force around them, like a magnetic field, and that the exact size of this field indicates the nature of the object: for example, a piece of brass or copper has a field exactly 61 inches across at ground level. Lethbridge adds that if you try to get above that field—by climbing on something—you cannot do it; the field extends upwards. He says: 'You cannot do so without a fireman's ladder,' and adds 'and perhaps you cannot do so then,' indicating that he hasn't tried it. In fact, if Robert Leftwich can dowse from an aeroplane, it seems probable that the field extends upwards for a very great distance—although, admittedly, he was dealing with vast quantities of mineral deposits. Lethbridge remarks that the size of the object seems to make no difference to the size of the field; a brass pinhead or a brass coin would still create a 61 inch field. This again suggests the need for further investigation, for it seems unlikely that a brass mountain would have a 61 inch field.

The dowser 'picks up' this field, as if he were a radio receiver. In an article 'More In Heaven and Earth,' published in the magazine of the British Society of Dowsers, Leftwich suggests that dowsing depends on 'high frequency electromagnetic waves' sent out from the dowser's brain like radar waves. In a second article in the same journal, he suggests that objects also emit waves, which are picked up by the dowser, and his final view would seem to be that the brain can emit 'radar' waves and that objects possess their own force field, hovering around it like the smell of gorgonzola cheese. (I will discuss his most recent thoughts on dowsing later in this chapter.)

Now this matter of 'fields' is of considerable interest, and it seems likely that this will be the direction of the real breakthrough in 'occult' researches. In 1845, Baron Karl Von Reichenbach published a book whose shortened title is *The Dynamics of Magnetism*. He was not discussing iron magnets, but the human magnetic field. Like the physician Anton Mesmer, Reichenbach believed that magnets (iron ones) might have healing properties. Neurasthenic patients—what he called 'sick sensitives'—were able to see light radiating from the poles of magnets—bluish from the north pole, reddish from the south. They lost this power when their health improved. As Reichenbach tested an increasing number of materials on his 'sick sensitives'—crystals, other metals—he found that they *all* seemed to possess a field of force. He called this force 'odile'; it became notorious as 'odic force.' He said that human beings possess odic force to an unusual degree, and it can be seen in the dark, streaming from the finger ends in the form of a light emanation.

For a decade and a half, scientists busily discussed and tested odic force. Then Darwin published *The Origin of Species* (1859). For a while, everything else was forgotten. And as scientists had to defend themselves against attacks from the church, they laid more and more emphasis on the scientific attitude—i.e. only believing what can be proved by observation. Reichenbach and his odic force were one of the earliest victims of this new attitude; twenty years after the publication of his book, his name—and ideas—had become a joke. Perhaps it was partly his own fault for choosing a term like odic force; if he had called it 'biomagnetic vibrations' or something of the sort, scientists might have continued to believe in it.

Almost a century later, in the late 1930s, a cranky and slightly paranoid man of genius, Wilhelm Reich, concluded that the universe is permeated by a kind of vital energy called orgone energy. At first, Reich was inclined to believe that this energy—which gave him conjunctivitis when he had been examining sea-sand culture under a microscope—was emitted by 'bions,' pulsating living cells, which he had observed some years earlier. One night, looking at the night sky through an improvised tube, he observed a flickering in the dark spaces between the stars, and concluded that the atmosphere is full of 'orgone energy.' His theory, roughly, is that this vital energy is present throughout the universe, and that it can actually create living cells even in a sterile fluid. Reich constructed a kind of greenhouse for concentrating this orgone energy—a box made of alternate layers of steel and asbestos (i.e. metal and organic material). I myself have sat in one of these boxes in the study of Reich's brother-in-law, the late Robert Ollen-

dorff, and experienced a distinct feeling of warmth—
although the walls were cold—and noted that my temperature rose by three degrees in a few minutes.

With ideas like this, it was inevitable that Reich
should be ridiculed by the scientific establishment. He
was; not only ridiculed, but attacked and persecuted.
When he died in prison in 1957, he had become distinctly paranoid and was suffering from delusions. The
general view was that it was good riddance; he was a
crank with messianic delusions, and was probably better
dead.

Now, nearly two decades after Reich's death, there is
reason to wonder whether both he and Reichenbach had
stumbled on something that orthodox science had overlooked—something as fundamental as Newton's discovery of the laws of gravity.

In 1935, before Reich discovered orgone energy, two
respectable American scientists, Dr. Harold Saxton Burr
and F. S. C. Northrop, both of Yale, published a paper
called 'Electro-dynamic Theory of Life,' suggesting,
quite simply, that living things produce electrical fields
that can be measured. And for the next three decades,
Burr and his colleagues continued to investigate these
'life fields' (or L-fields, as Edward Russell has pro-
posed we call them). The first problem was to develop a
voltmeter sensitive enough to measure very small fields;
but once this was done, it was plain sailing. The voltmeters were connected up to a couple of large trees for
years, and they showed that the electrical field of the
trees varied between day and night, and with electrical
storms and sun spots. Animals were more problematic,
since they cannot be made to stand still for years; but
Burr soon discovered that there are variations in the
body's magnetic field when we are ill, when wounds are
healing, when women ovulate. (This last discovery ap-

parently provides a more or less infallible guide for parents who want children. And the discovery of body variations in periods of illness indicates a method for the early detection of cancer.)

In the sixties, European and American doctors became increasingly interested in the ancient Chinese medical practice known as acupuncture. By all western standards, this ought to be unscientific nonsense; but it works. It was originally based on the observation that when someone is ill, his skin often develops 'tender points' and that pressure applied to these points seems to improve the illness. The theory behind the acupuncture is that the universe is permeated with various vital forces—like the 'lines of power' mentioned in John Michell's *View Over Atlantis*—and that the same vital forces permeate the human body, with definite crossing points like 'leys.' This vital energy is called Qi or Ch'i (breath). A television film shown in England early in 1973 showed doctors performing operations that would usually require anaesthesia, with the patient fully conscious, and a few wooden slivers sticking out of various points of the body. The patient was able to watch his own stomach being cut open, see it sewed up, and apparently take it all very calmly. (Recovery also seemed to be incredibly fast—some patients were eating large meals a few hours after serious operations.)

In Russia, acupuncture is used nearly as much as in China. And a Russian scientist, Victor Adamenko, developed a device called a tobioscope to establish acupuncture points. Adamenko's starting point was a device invented thirty or so years ago by two scientists, Semyon and Valentina Kirlian. This consists of a Telsa coil—a transformer for high frequency alternating currents, used in radio—which is connected to two metal plates. Between these plates, an object—alive or otherwise—is placed in contact with a piece of film, then the high frequency current is switched on. The result is a photograph of the 'field' of the object. For example, if a newly cut flower is placed between the plates, light can be seen streaming from the cut stem in the form of 'sparks,' while leaves and buds show flare patterns. Photographs of the human body show the same flare patterns, and Stanley Krippner, an American scientist who examined these photographs in Russia (and wrote about them in an article in the *Saturday Evening Post*, 18 March 1972), comments that they change if the subject is hypnotised, takes drugs or drinks alcohol. This suggests that they are nodes of energy. And since acupuncture theory has it that these 'meridional' points can be blocked with too much energy, it seems possible that the camera is recording such points. (Everyone must have noticed that some point of the skin may suddenly 'prickle'—sometimes as if a needle is being driven in; you only have to start thinking about this to get 'prickles' on the skin—presumably due to some kind of discharge of nervous energy, like static.)

Obviously, it is no great scientific problem to convert the light energy—as observed by the Kirlian device—into electrical energy, and this is what Victor Adamenko has done in his tobioscope. It is a kind of flashlight that is passed over the patient's skin, and which goes on and off as it passes over acupuncture points. If the patient is healthy, it gives a good light; if unhealthy, it is dim. The relation to Harold Burr's work on 'life fields' is obvious. (For example, sunspots affect the Kirlian photographs.) Kirlian photographs have been taken of the whole body; one of Mrs. Kulagina, an adept in psychokinesis, shows a pulsating field around the body. (Mrs. Kulagina is, apparently, able to move objects like matches and paperclips by passing her hands close to them; Stanley

Krippner reports that she has even made them move by thought alone.)

It certainly looks, then, as though a century after Reichenbach, the reality of his odic force (read: 'field of force') is being demonstrated. Which makes it seem that dowsing, even in its odder manifestations, is as explainable as any other simple wave phenomena. We simply need an Isaac Newton of this new field to recognise the underlying laws of the phenomena. I'm inclined to believe that Lethbridge has taken the largest step in this direction so far. In *Ghost and Divining-Rod,* he advances the theory that there are specific electrical fields connected with water (including the sea), and with mountains and deserts; and although he chooses to call these by romantic names such as 'naiad fields,' 'oread fields' and 'nereid fields,' he regards them as perfectly normal electrical fields. He observed that 'ghost' and 'ghoul' phenomena often seem to occur in the area of such fields. For example, he saw a 'ghost' at Hole Mill, near Seaton, and discovered that an underground stream connected the spot where he was standing with the spot where he saw the ghost. At which point, he makes a further assumption: that his own 'psychic field' was able to pick up a *picture* implanted on the 'naiad field' of the stream by the 'ghost's' psychic field many years before. In other words, that the 'ghost' was really a kind of snapshot, imprinted on the naiad field by some intense emotion. (He suggests that intense happiness can 'imprint' itself on 'fields' just as easily as intense misery or fear.) The same applies to the 'ghouls' he has sensed on various occasions—for example, on Ladram beach.*

* A similar theory was developed in a television play by Nigel Kneale, *The Stone Tape,* broadcast over Christmas 1972. The 'stone tape' refers to the walls of a building in which some horrifying event has taken place in the remote past. Again, the suggestion is that ghosts are not living entities, just 'recordings.'

In his book *Design for Destiny* (Neville Spearman, 1971), Edward Russell, an American journalist, quotes Burr's experiments with 'life fields,' and then goes on to cite the results of the Russian scientist L. L. Vasiliev, professor of physiology at Leningrad, who performed a series of experiments that demonstrated the reality of telepathy beyond all reasonable doubt. Vasiliev had two subjects sitting in different rooms; one sent out suggestions that the other should fall asleep. It worked. Moreover, it worked over immense distances—from Leningrad to Sevastopol, and it worked even if the subjects were enclosed in a metal chamber that would prevent any transmission by electrical fields. Vasiliev's extremely detailed and complicated experiments were published in a book called *Experiments in Mental Suggestion,* which has so far been published in England only in a limited edition. Mr. Russell argues that these experiments prove the existence of another kind of field, 'thought fields,' which he calls T-fields. He goes on to state that T-fields can 'attach themselves to any kind of matter.' He is speaking about Lethbridge's 'ghouls' and such like: 'Many an estate agent, trying to sell a desirable property, must have been puzzled and disappointed when clients exclaimed: "Ugh, let's get out of here! This place gives me the willies!" He adds that the size of the object on which the field is impressed seems to make no difference: it can be as large as a house or as small as a pinhead. An observation that brings to mind Lethbridge's remark about the constant size of electrical fields for various metals, and again suggests that we are here dealing with some general law concerning fields.

Another important clue is offered in the book called *The World of Ted Serios* by Dr. Jule Eisenbud (which I have also discussed in *The Occult*). Ted Serios is an alcoholic bellboy who has the extraordinary ability to press a Polaroid camera against his head, and somehow imprint 'mental photographs' on the plate. The photographs, many of which are included in the book, are usually of places. Eisenbud was shocked when he discovered that, although Serios's results seemed genuine, no one was interested. He need not have been surprised. The problem is that Serios's powers do not fit into any general pattern. It is like a piece of a jigsaw puzzle that doesn't connect together with any other piece. So, for the time being, it is pushed to a corner of the table and left alone; no one is interested in it until some interlocking pieces can be found. And this is again demonstrated by the fate of the book; it excited a good deal of interest when it appeared; since when, it seems to have lapsed into relative oblivion. But some of the interlocking pieces may perhaps be found in Lethbridge and the Kirlian device. The Kirlian device takes photographs of life fields, or psychic fields, proving they can be impressed on a photographic plate; Ted Serios can impress his 'T-fields' on a photographic plate. And, Lethbridge suggests, any human beings may impress a T-field on the electrical field associated with a certain area, particularly if that area has water running through it.

I was already aware of the probable importance of 'fields' in explaining psychic phenomena before I met Robert Leftwich. So I found most of his ideas and theories easy enough to accept. I had an opportunity to explore these further a few months after that first meeting. In January 1972, I became one of the presenters of a monthly arts programme, *Format*, on Westward Television. In May 1972, Michael Joseph brought out a book called *The Table Rappers*, a history of spiritualism by Ronald Pearsall, who lives in the west country. Mr. Pearsall's point of view is distinctly sceptical; so when I asked him to appear on the programme, I also asked

Robert Leftwich if he would care to take part. He agreed, and drove down to Cornwall on the day of the programme. It was an interesting discussion. I asked Leftwich to explain about 'astral projection'; he said that he could only do it at certain times, which seem to come around periodically. He can feel it 'coming on' for some days in advance. He described how, on one occasion, he had been sitting on the London Underground, feeling rather oppressed by the crowds; so he closed his eyes— to look as if he was asleep—and 'projected' himself out of his body. After a while someone noticed him; his face had gone very pale, and he seemed to have stopped breathing. There was a minor panic; but while the passengers were discussing what to do with the corpse, Robert arrived at his station, opened his eyes, and walked off the train. . . .

The story is typical; it demonstrates the element of schoolboyish mischief that is a definite part of Leftwich's make-up. It seems incongruous; but this is because most of us have formed our conceptions about 'psychic powers' from fairy stories; from the *Arabian Nights* to Tolkien's *Lord of the Rings,* the wizards have grey beards, piercing eyes and a basilisk-like stare. The truth is that psychic powers are almost accidental; their possessors may belong to any personality type. This is particularly true in the case of 'astral projection,' also known as 'out-of-the-body experience' (and ecsomatic experience). They often seem to occur by accident, if one can accept the testimony of those who claim to have experienced it. For example, in *Out-of-the Body Experiences* by Celia Green (Vol. II of the Proceedings of the Institute of Psychophysical Research, Oxford, 1968), a waitress describes how she was walking home in a state of fatigue when she suddenly realised that her body was *below* her, walking along the street; a girl reading a book suddenly found herself floating near the ceiling, looking down on her body in the chair; a man sitting on the seat of a bus suddenly found himself on the stairs, looking at himself still seated. The two classic books on the subject are *The Phenomena of Astral Projection* (1951), and *The Projection of the Astral Body* (1929), both by Sylvan Muldoon and Hereward Carrington, and I must refer the reader to these for further information.

I had been hoping to carry out some systematic exploration of Robert Leftwich's 'strange powers' when he came to see us in Cornwall; but again, I was disappointed. This was not his fault. He seemed willing to discuss any subject frankly; but his ideas about his powers are bound up with ideas about vegetarianism, health foods, marriage, morality, and so on. So a question about the first time he experienced astral projection might produce a discourse on his diet, childhood fantasies, army experiences or marriage.

When I had been at Beacon House, he had shown me the typescript of a 'book,' actually a volume of essays, called *The Philosophy of an Escapist;* I had been puzzled by the title, until he explained that by 'escapist,' he meant someone who wanted to escape the rat-race and retire to a place where he could meditate. I had wanted to borrow the typescript, but it was the only one and he was unwilling to let it out of his hands. Now he brought me a photocopy to Cornwall, and I had a chance to study it in more detail. I found it an immensely interesting document, which provided me with a great deal more insight into his character; but as far as explaining his 'powers' was concerned, it was again a disappointment. All the same, it did provide certain insights. It was clear from the opening paragraphs that Leftwich is a typical 'outsider' figure. 'The idea of settling down away from the influences of modern civilisation and its appalling artificiality originated in my mind almost immediately after I left College. . . .' An 'outsider,' in the terminology I developed, is a self-actualiser who wants to side-step the demands of everyday life and get down to creation. He (or she) wants to evolve, to move on. Maslow's classic case was of a girl who had been a brilliant sociology student at college, and was forced to take a job as a personnel manager in a chewing gum factory during the depression years; she became so depressed she even ceased to menstruate. Maslow cured her by simply suggesting that she should continue her studies at night school. She was getting sick of marking time, staying in the same place. W. B. Yeats had a fantasy of a 'Castle on a Rock' where a community of poets and artists could spend their lives growing vegetables and living the life of the mind. What really destroyed Van Gogh was not the mental strain of being a visionary; it was the strain of never knowing where his next meal was coming from, of always being poor, of having to live off his brother, who, unburdened by a powerful creative urge, was able to bring himself to work for a living. Gauguin hoped to find his freedom in the South Seas, but poverty followed him there. *This* is the basic problem of the Outsider; he just wants *time* to sort himself out, to be creative.

In my own teens, I dreamed of retiring to one of those stone huts on the Aran Isles, formerly occupied by religious ascetics. This problem—of how to stay alive and develop my potentialities, in a society that insisted that I work forty-five hours a week for just enough maney to keep me alive—was solved by the success of *The Outsider*. It is true that it brought as many problems as it solved; but it certainly solved that basic problem: of how to avoid working in a factory or office, doing somebody else's business instead of my own. So I had solved the problem by the time I was twenty-four. The writer's life still has plenty of problems—*The Author* has conducted a survey that showed that less than a hundred writers in Great Britain can live wholly from their writing—but at least they are problems you can feel strongly about, not problems that strike you as infinitely boring and irrelevant.

Robert Leftwich had faced the problem logically, and set out to solve it in a sensible, determined way: to save enough money to retire while fairly young, and be able to devote the last third of his life to 'self-actualisation.' 'I began to economise very enthusiastically by depriving myself of all unnecessary luxuries. . . .' I had had a shot at the same method, working for a few weeks to make a little spare money, then sleeping out in a sleeping bag to save rent, and eating in cheap workman's cafés. I also had reason to sympathise with Robert's divagation, if that is the word: '. . . ultimately, the basic desire for female companionship superseded these food intentions, with the result that . . . I eventually found myself engaged.' I had also found myself married and a parent; I fled the dilemma, rather than solved it, by separating from my wife after eighteen months. Robert had behaved more decently; he married, produced children, and continued to work towards the ideal of 'escape,' while continuing to take full responsibility for his wife and children. He had recognized, after a while, that marriage and parenthood would not provide a substitute for what he really wanted. When I first met him, he felt he had about another year before he could 'escape'; at the time of writing, two years later, he is somewhere in the South of France with a caravan, while Patricia and the children are in England.

The desire for escape has been Leftwich's lifelong preoccupation. And it suggests a reason for the development of his unusual powers. He set himself a long-dis-

tance aim—a *very* long-distance aim, since it has taken
him until he is fifty to achieve it. Now, anybody who has
ever set out determinedly to lose weight knows about
the curious effect of 'moral uplift' that can come from
self-discipline. Once you've embarked on the course,
and see your weight vanishing at a rate of five pounds
a week, you become a kind of miser about every mouth-
ful of bread. You begin to calculate—by Easter you'll
have lost twenty-five pounds. . . . Being hungry becomes
a kind of pleasure. It even becomes a kind of addiction;
doctors are familiar with cases of girls who diet to
achieve 'Twiggy figures,' and then continue to starve
until they are suffering from serious undernourishment,
and have to be force-fed. But even dieting is a fairly
short-term discipline; at the end of three months or so,
you can go back to normal eating. Robert Leftwich has
been subjecting himself to a rigorous self-discipline for
twenty-five years or so.

Now, what does discipline *do*? Basically, it increases
one's 'vital reserves'—or, rather, makes them more
available. It makes one more 'free.' Sartre said he had
never felt so free as during the war, when he was in the
Resistance, was likely to be arrested and shot at any moment. Why? Because he had to maintain a higher level
of alertness, of 'preparedness.' Similarly, the disciplines
evolved by Gurdjieff—and practised at his Institute for
the Harmonious Development of Man at Fontainebleau
—aimed at keeping his pupils in a state of constant alertness: they might be asked to leap out of bed in the
middle of the night and instantly assume some difficult
position. A young boy, Fritz Peters, was induced to
make greater and greater efforts mowing the lawns, until
he could do vast areas in one day. The aim was to keep
everyone bubbling with energy. 'Compared to what we
ought to be, we are only half awake,' said William

James, who might almost have been quoting Gurdjieff. (Gurdjieff would have said that, compared to what we ought to be, we are fast asleep.) 'We are making use of only a small part of our mental and physical resources.' 'We live subject to arrest by degrees of fatigue which we have come only from habit to obey. Most of us may learn to push the barrier further off, and to live in perfect comfort on much higher levels of power.' And he adds: 'The transformation, moreover, is a chronic one; the new level of energy becomes permanent.' All these quotations are from his important essay 'The Energies of Man.'

It is not only ignorance—or laziness—that keeps us 'below our proper selves.' All animals are complicated systems of drives *and* inhibitions. Different circumstances require different responses. In battle, it is of great advantage to be carried away by anger; in peace time, it could be a great disadvantage. A self-controlled man would be able to *allow* himself to be carried away by anger when it suits him, and to inhibit it when it doesn't: that is to say, he sets up a system of control even over the ability to lose control. Such complexities are bound to defeat their own purpose sometimes—particularly in modern civilised life: hence Rousseau's nostalgia for the life of the noble savage; hence the rising rate of neurosis in our society. The sheer entanglement of inhibitory systems and anti-inhibitory systems and systems for overruling anti-inhibitory systems is bound to produce a certain energy wastage through tension. Psychologists have observed that when a patient is hypnotised, and told that he cannot move his arm, he finds it impossible to move it, no matter how hard he tries. On examining what is happening in more detail, it has been found that, for example, a patient who has been told to bend his arm is actually contracting his flexor muscles, but is also contracting the extensor muscles to prevent him from bending it; his self-division (in this case, an artificial one caused by the hypnotist) causes him to *cancel out* an action he is attempting to perform. On the other hand, tests on patients under hypnosis have also shown that they can be made to exert far more strength than they are capable of exerting when 'awake': up to one-third more. Their mental performance can also be improved in a similar ratio. We might say, then, that our natural powers are inhibited by a self-consciousness that has the same basic nature as embarrassment or stage fright. I can overcome this 'cancelling' process in two ways: either by relaxing completely (perhaps with the aid of drugs or alcohol, or by meditation techniques), or by making such a steady and determined effort that I launch myself onto a higher plane of energy, in which the forward drive completely overrules the inhibitory mechanism.

In his book, Leftwich says he isn't sure whether his tireless energy is due to his 'self-imposed restrictive way of life,' or whether he was 'fortunate enough to inherit a very high basic metabolic rate.' I would plump for the first.

I read a great deal of *Philosophy of an Escapist* that first night he stayed with us, and it was then that I definitely decided that I would like to write about him, whether or not I could satisfy my curiosity about his powers. I have to admit that I had misgivings about having Robert actually around the premises. I usually write all day; then, at six o'clock, I'm ready to pour a glass of wine and spend a long evening listening to music or reading, or even watching TV if there is some culturally reward- ing programme such as *Maigret* or *The Avengers*. I like to 'switch off' and become purely receptive; and I tend to resent it if I have guests who want to discuss questions of philosophy or psychology; it may be relaxation for them, but for me, it is talking shop. But Robert wasn't as bad as I'd anticipated. I was amused to watch Joy's reaction to him; I could see she didn't quite know what to make of him, bewildered by the impact of his school-boy exuberance and completely nonoffensive—because totally candid—egoism. He repeated some of the things he had said to me before—for example, about dowsing, or the ability to make things happen—and I noted that he repeated them in almost exactly the same words. This reinforced my feeling of his basic honesty; a man who is letting his imagination run away with him tends to change things slightly each time, to embroider. . . .

This ability to make things happen was, in effect, an extension of his trick of making the schoolmaster ask him to repeat the only lines he'd learned, and I found one story particularly interesting. Robert said he'd been talking with a friend about the power of the mind. They were walking through central London, and Robert said: 'For example, we could walk into any shop and take anything without paying for it.' When his friend showed scepticism, he offered to demonstrate. They walked into a shop that had two assistants. As they did so, one assistant said, 'I'm going to the storeroom,' and went out. At that moment, the telephone rang, and the other assistant said, 'Excuse me,' and also went out, leaving them alone. Robert said, 'You see.' 'But that's just coinci-dence,' said his friend. 'All right, I'll do it again.' They went into another shop. Within a few minutes, they were the only customers; then a delivery lorry arrived, and the assistant went out. . . . By this time the friend was looking worried. 'It's still coincidence. . . .' 'All right, we'll do it again.' And they did. Each time, by way of clinching his point, Robert took some small and inexpensive object, which he later gave away.

If this story sounded astonishing, his next statement was even more so. In order to establish beyond all doubt that this was a 'power' of the mind he was using, he decided to do it a *thousand* times. And he claims he did. He didn't say how long this took him, but he did mention that he devoted his 'proceeds,' such as they were, to charity.

No doubt this anecdote will arouse more scepticism than any so far. I find it consistent with Leftwich's other premises. There can be no doubt that the chief fault we have developed, through the long course of human evolution, is a certain basic *passivity*. When provoked by challenges, human beings are magnificent. When life is quiet and even, we take the path of least resistance, and then wonder why we feel bored. A man who is determined and active doesn't pay much attention to 'luck.' If things go badly, he takes a deep breath and redoubles his effort. And he quickly discovers that his moments of deepest happiness often come after such efforts. The man who has become accustomed to a passive existence becomes preoccupied with 'luck'; it may become an obsession. When things go well, he is delighted and good-humoured; when they go badly, he becomes gloomy and petulant. He is unhappy—or dissatisfied—most of the time, for even when he has no cause for complaint, he feels that gratitude would be premature; things might go wrong at any moment; you can't really trust the world. . . . Gambling is one basic response to this passivity, revealing the obsession with luck, the desire to make things happen.

The absurdity about this attitude is that we fail to recognize the active part we play in making life a pleasure. When my will is active, my whole mental and physical being *works* better, just as my digestion works better if I take exercise between meals. I gain an increasing feeling of control over my life, instead of the feeling of helplessness (what Sartre calls 'contingency') that comes from long periods of passivity. Yet even people who are intelligent enough to recognize this find the habit of passivity so deeply ingrained that they find themselves holding their breath when things go well, hoping fate will continue to be kind.

To actually believe, as Leftwich does, that *you* control your luck, could be a vital step in human evolution, a real turning point. And what is especially important is that he rejects the idea that you can 'push your luck' too far. He believes that this power to make things go well is as straightforward as any other physical activity. When a man sets out to drive to his office, he doesn't take a deep breath and say: 'Well, here goes. Let's hope I make it today. . . .' There *is* a chance that he may not make it, especially in modern city traffic; but he also knows that if he drives carefully enough, he'll make it. He doesn't even think: 'There's a ten thousand to one chance I might meet with an accident.' He simply takes it for granted that he'll reach his office. A little late, perhaps, if the traffic is bad; but he'll get there. So Leftwich's assertion that he decided to repeat his performance a thousand times, to *prove* that the mind can control 'luck,' is of some importance. He has laid down a basic principle of the next step in human evolution.

In *The Occult,* I quote a remark Robert Graves made to me: that many young men use a form of witchcraft to seduce young women. I had been instantly struck by the truth of this. My own experience has not been wide or varied, but I knew exactly what he meant. A man wants a girl, and he begins to *think about her* in a particular way; not just daydreaming, but with a kind of calculating determination, like a hunter who is determined to get a certain animal if he has to track it for weeks. Some kind of psychic force seems to come into operation—*connected with imagination,* just like the trick of turning the paper roundabout—and he may feel certain that he'll achieve his object long before he has any concrete reasons for thinking so.

Leftwich's power to 'make things happen' is an extension of this. I am inclined to believe that it involves no 'occult' faculty (such as second sight): that it is a power that depends simply on calling upon our 'vital reserves' and abandoning the customary attitude of passivity.

Leftwich has visited me twice in Cornwall—the second time early in 1973. He had finally resigned from his job, bought himself a dormobile, and was prepared to take up his 'life of freedom' at last. He showed us the dormobile, and all its gadgets; these included a generator that, at the touch of a switch, would cause six thousand volts to surge through the bodywork of the vehicle. A sensible precaution, perhaps: no doubt a man who has slept in a house most of his life feels insecure if he parks at the side of the road in some remote part of France—perhaps remembering the fate of the Drummond family. . . . But also typical of Robert Leftwich, with that schoolboy delight in gadgets.

From my own experience of him, I can vouch that he never seems to get tired—at least, not noticeably. At seven in the morning, as Joy was sleepily switching on the kettle and preparing to get the children's breakfast, Robert would appear outside the kitchen window, as chirpy as if he'd been for a ten-mile walk, looking for

the shredded wheat and eager to elaborate on some point
that he'd overlooked the night before. . . . He also seems
to possess the ability to prevent himself from getting
cold. I find I need a fairly even temperature; if the
room gets cool, I begin to feel chilly around the neck,
and need a scarf; if my workroom gets too warm, I have
to change my woollen sweater for a cotton one. Robert always seemed to be dressed in the same clothes—a
sports jacket, shirt and tie, flannel trousers—and to be
unaffected by temperature. He explained that it had
struck him one day that when you are embarrassed, you
go 'hot all over,' and that this power to increase one's
body temperature must be natural to man. Ever since
that time, he says, he has been able to increase his
bodily temperature at will.

It was during the first visit to Cornwall that I set the
tape recorder going, and started asking him questions.
What I wanted chiefly was a straightforward biograph-
ical outline. The following is a brief summary of what
he told me.

The Leftwich family is basically French, originating
in Saint-Sauveur in northern France; the family name
was originally De Leftwyche. Since his mother was
also French, Robert Leftwich may be regarded as more
than 50 per cent Gallic. The family moved to North-
wich, where there was, at one time, a Leftwich Hall.
On the whole, then, the family 'came down in the
world.' Even so, his father, a mathematician and member of the Royal Society, had some distinguished
friends, including Sir James Jeans, Sir Arthur Eddington and Sir Charles Boyes, the man who 'weighed the
earth.' Robert's rather casual relationship with the last
ended when he was eleven or twelve; Sir Charles invited the Leftwich family to his home near Andover.
Wandering around the garden, Robert found a pump.

Even at this time, he was fascinated by hydraulic devices. He primed the pump with a bucket of water, and worked the handle. A sludgy substance came out. He assumed the pump needed a lot more working before clear water came through, so he went on pumping. . . . In fact, he emptied the liquid manure tanks, and flooded the lawn. Sir Charles wrote Leftwich senior a letter, asking him not to bring his son to the house in future. . . .

Fortunately, his father was a patient man—he needed to be with a son who was a born rebel and always into mischief. (At this point, Robert made an interesting digression. He himself, he says, is not a particularly good or patient father. 'I love my children, but I don't really like them. Because, I suppose, they're too much like me—rebellious. Particularly Bobby. Which is largely my own fault. I decided I wanted to have a child with the same birthday as myself. So my wife and I did calculations. In fact, Bobby arrived a few hours after my birthday—16 May—was over. But if there's anything in astrology—our characters are almost identical.'*)

Robert may have inherited some of his 'psychic' fac-

---

* I must admit that I never cease to be amazed at the weird accuracy of astrological character assessments. According to Derek Parker's *The Compleat Astrologer*, the character of the Taurean—21 April to 21 May—is 'Practical, reliable, adept at business, having strong powers of endurance, a firm sense of values.' Negative traits may include possessiveness and an obsession with routines. 'He will be likely to be successful in a career to do with finance, and he will look forward to security (with pension) in retirement. . . . At the same time, he has a distinct artistic leaning.' As to the relation with his children: 'It is very difficult for the Taurean, with his very conservative instincts, to bridge the generation gap with the young; and all too easy for him, with his liking for discipline, to ignore the fact that his children may not be in sympathy with his ideas. . . .'

ulties from his mother; she was the sort of person who could say at breakfast 'I've got a feeling I'm going to hear from so and so today'—and the postman would then arrive with the letter. But on the whole, there was nothing psychic about his family; it was a matter that simply did not interest them. So when, at the age of four or five, Robert found himself one evening looking down on his own body in the bed, there was no one in the family who could explain to him that he was simply experiencing 'astral projection.' Children take these things much more for granted than adults, so this odd ability never worried him. He was certainly not one of Reichenbach's 'sick sensitives.' In fact, his account of himself as a child makes him sound more like Richmal Crompton's Just William, with a touch of Jefferies' Bevis. He played elaborate imaginative games with a close friend, and they encouraged one another in such dangerous feats as dropping off a railway bridge on to the moving carriages below. This adventurous 'Just William' element continues to be a strong part of his character; later on, he travelled thousands of miles around Europe and North Africa on the tops of trains, or, occasionally, clinging underneath the carriages.

In spite of his self-discipline, his attention to detail, Leftwich is basically an anarchist. 'I can't bear any form of regimentation.' Listening to his anecdotes, I was suddenly reminded of Gurdjieff. In his autobiographical book *Meetings with Remarkable Men*, Gurdjieff emerges as an amiable rogue. He spent the first half of his life wandering from place to place—'bumming around,' as we would say now—making a living as best he could; his methods were usually ingenious, sometimes downright crooked. And yet, beyond all shadow of doubt, he was no charlatan; he possessed knowledge and he possessed power. In many ways,

Robert's personality make-up resembles Gurdjieff's. It suddenly struck me that these anecdotes about his anti-authoritarianism, his obsession with travel, are not as irrelevant as I at first thought. He was telling me a story about an RAF driving instructor who was supposed to teach him to drive a truck. Robert could already drive, so when the man began to explain, 'This is the ignition key, this is the clutch,' he became impatient. When he started the truck, he went from first, into second, then into third gear. At which the instructor stopped him with a roar of rage. 'If you don't do as you're told we'll never get anywhere.' 'But I *can* drive.' 'As far as I'm concerned, you can't. Now, let's start again. This is the ignition key. . . .' One can understand his reaction in the face of this kind of unbelievable stupidity. On the other hand, it reinforced the individualism, the determination to go his own way and to stand alone. And this, in turn, encouraged the development of this odd power 'to make things happen.' 'Witchcraft,' of the kind we have been discussing, depends on clearly *wanting* something, and directing all your psychic energies towards getting it. Robert's clashes with authority in its most obtuse and bigoted form led him to form a very clear idea that he wanted freedom: the first necessity for obtaining it.

His RAF career offers some excellent examples of the working of 'Leftwichcraft.' The war was over—fortunately—when he was posted abroad. On the boat to Dieppe, the sea was rough, and the washrooms were full of vomiting men. Robert wanted to use the toilet; so he marched around the deck until he came to a sign 'Out of bounds to all ranks,' and unhesitatingly went past it. The crew allowed him to use their toilet, and then invited him to join them in a game of cards; he had actually won 7/6d when the boat arrived in France.

Then there was a long rail journey south. It suddenly struck Robert that he was approaching the country of his ancestors, and that he had relatives in Cannes. In the transit camp, all was confusion. So he buried his kit-bag, and walked out. In Cannes, fortunately, there were no military police. He found his relatives, lived there for a couple of months, then finally made his way back to the camp. He dug up his kitbag and found himself a bed. The next day on parade, names were called from a list. Robert reasoned that no one was checking on each individual, so he picked up his kitbag and joined the group who were due to leave. At the docks, they were counted and found to be one too many. The last man on the list was sent back. Robert went on to North Africa, and found himself in the camp that con-tained the remaining men of his old unit—the rest had already been posted all over the Middle East. A couple of days after that, his own name was called out on parade, and he was posted. No one had even noticed his absence.

Instead of thanking his stars that he'd avoided a court martial, Robert continued to 'push his luck.' He was assigned to the job of driving the 'shit wagon'; he didn't like it. So on the second day, he refused. It should have resulted in being put on a charge; instead, after being interviewed by everyone from the MT officer to the Wing Commander in charge of the station, he was tem-porarily taken off duty. Then he was offered the job of helping to reclaim and recondition vehicles that had broken down in the desert during the war, and a team of engineers to help him do it. Once again, he had the freedom he wanted. One day, he was told to take a Daimler to Cairo, and to instruct the chauffeur of Sir Charles Medhurst, Commander in Chief in the Middle East, in how to drive it. It struck Robert that this was the kind of job he would enjoy. In this case, his 'Left-wichcraft' was facilitated by the fact that Sir Charles had known his Aunt Vera Leftwich. He became Medhurst's chauffeur; and eventually, with a certain amount of string-pulling (involving Aunt Vera), he obtained his discharge from the forces.

By this time, his direction was fixed, although he still had a long way to go before understanding what it was he wanted out of life. He knew he wanted to travel; he also experienced an obscurer need, a desire to understand his own inner-being, which took the form of intense curiosity about world religions. He went back to the Middle East, to study Mahommedanism at first hand; he also used his childhood knowledge to travel long distances without paying. (On one occasion, travelling from Cairo to Haifa on the roof of a train, he came close to being decapitated. He was standing up on the roof, stretching and yawning, when the friend with whom he was travelling dragged him down; the telegraph wires crossed from one side of the track to the other, about five feet above the roof of the train. . . .) Like Sir Richard Burton, he disguised himself as an Arab and went into mosques. He saw nothing that convinced him that his answer lay in Islam. The interest in religion disposed his mind more favourably to Christianity (to which his attitude had always been lukewarm), although he found the 'middle of the road' doctrines of the Church of England uninteresting. The millennialism of the Seventh Day Adventists appealed altogether more strongly: their conviction of the imminence of the Second Coming, their absorption in the prophecies of the Old Testament; even their Sabbatarian Fundamentalism appealed to the ascetic side of him. But after a while, he found himself unable to stomach the dogmatism, and turned to the study of religions of the east—Hinduism and Buddhism. He was also unable to accept the idea of Jesus as the God-Man and Saviour, and declined to accept that the miracles proved his divinity. He already had a suspicion that anyone can perform miracles if he can tap his hidden resources. Nevertheless, the Seventh Day Adventists were an important influence, with their emphasis on the importance of physical health, their sparing use of meat and intense dislike of tobacco and alcohol. (I asked Robert if he had always been a non-smoker. He said No; he had smoked as a young man. One day in a cinema, he realised he was out of cigarettes, and felt such a strong desire for a smoke that he went out to the foyer to buy some. Back in the cinema, he began to brood on his dependence on cigarettes—even then he believed that the mind should be able to completely control the body. He got up, left the cinema, presented the cigarettes to the first man he met in the street, and gave up smoking.)

On the whole, Buddhism struck him as the religion that made the strongest appeal to his inner needs; he still regards himself as fundamentally a Buddhist (although, in the *Philosophy of an Escapist,* he states his belief in a Creator of the universe, and seems altogether closer to a mystical pantheism). During this stage—when he was investigating comparative religion—he had no particular interest in 'occultism.' I asked him if he could say roughly when it began to interest him. He placed the date at about 1957, when he was looking around an antique shop near Reigate. He got into conversation with the proprietor, a woman, and when he left, shook her hand. She looked at him in an odd way, and said, 'You're a healer, aren't you?' Robert said not as far as he knew. She looked at his hand, and what she saw in his palm apparently confirmed her intuition; she told him that he had a line on his palm that only one person in ten thousand possesses.

Still, he was sceptical—or perhaps only uninterested. Five more years went by. One morning, on his way to work, he noticed workmen digging a hole; on the previous two days he had noticed them digging holes in other places nearby. He stopped the car and asked them what they were doing ('You know I'm extremely inquisitive'). They said they'd lost the water main—and at that moment, a diviner arrived, took out his rods, and within a few minutes had located the main. Robert asked if he could try it, and the diviner handed him the forked stick. Robert walked over the main—and felt the stick twist violently in his hands. He was so excited that he decided not to go to work. Instead, he went to the Lewes Public Library, and consulted all their books on dowsing. He discovered that there is a British Society of Dowsers, and that the president was a Colonel Bell who lived in Cookfield. Robert contacted him, and soon became an active dowser. At the same time, he discovered he also possessed certain healing gifts—someone told him that dowsing and healing go together. (He has never tried to develop these; but he can cure his wife of severe migraine in a few minutes, by laying his hands on her forehead; and can cure an ordinary headache in ten seconds.)

When Brian Inglis came to lecture to the Society, he asked if any dowsers would be willing to demonstrate their powers on television. Everyone declined; the general feeling was that these things depend on a certain inner-concentration, and that TV cameras would spoil it. Robert said this was untrue. If dowsing depended on the power of the mind, then it shouldn't make any difference where it was done.

The result was the TV broadcast of 1968 when—as

already mentioned—he found three out of five tins of water, a result he regarded as poor, but which satisfied Brian Inglis—as well as the Society of Dowsers, who had declined to have anything to do with the programme.

Having discovered that he could dowse for water, Leftwich was curious to know what other hidden abilities he might possess. Experiment soon convinced him that he could find anything—provided he had an idea of what he was looking for. He can detect any liquid—for example, oil—any solid object, and even empty space (he has often been asked to dowse for tunnels). This obviously suggests that he has some subconscious knowledge of the 'field' he is looking for. Again, it is the 'directionality' of the mind that seems to be important. Most of us lack these abilities because we never direct the mind in that direction.

He also seems to possess strong telepathic abilities, although these depend, to a large extent, upon whether the other person involved is a good receiver (or transmitter). He mentioned one friend who is an exceptionally good receiver. Robert hands him a pack of cards, tells him to shuffle them, and then place several cards, face downward, on a table. He says: 'Move your hand back and forward over the cards; the one you finally decide to pick up will be the ten of diamonds.' His friend moves his hand, hesitates, then says: 'No, I won't have that one—I'll have this. . . .' And his second choice proves to be the ten of diamonds. The friend often asks: 'How did you do that?' to which Robert replies: 'I don't know.'

I felt this *was* an area in which I could test him. (I had contemplated getting him to accompany me round the local shops, and getting him to demonstrate his powers of shoplifting; but it struck me that if he failed,

we might both be in trouble.) We took a pack of cards
—it was ours, not his. He told me to shuffle them, and
then start placing them, face down, on the table, while
he stood several feet away, where he could not see the
cards. 'I'll stop you when you get to the ace of clubs.'
After I had thrown down twenty cards or so, he said:
'Stop, that's it.' It was the ace of clubs. We did it several times more. He was not right every time—I think
there were three failures out of seven. He was apolo-
getic, and said that it could be because this was the first
time we'd tried it; but I found the performance impressive.

On the other hand, I have to admit that, in spite of his
obvious dowsing abilities, his demonstration in that direction was not wholly successful either. When he came
to see us in 1972, I was having water trouble. To begin with, I noticed that the walls of a new room we'd
just had built on to the house were getting damp at the
bottom. One day, I moved a bookcase and found the
floor, and carpet, underneath it flooded. With the help
of the local handyman—who built the room—I knocked
a hole in the outside wall, just below ground level. As
the chisel went through, there was a violent gush of
water, and a torrent came from under the house. When
we turned off the water at the main, the flood ceased;
obviously, we had a burst pipe. The problem: to locate
the burst, and dig down to it. It had to be exactly located, unless I wanted to tear up several yards of concrete. Robert walked around the room, and got strong
water reactions from near the far wall. (Oddly enough,
so did Joy, who asked if she could try his rods—she is
obviously another natural dowser.) He wandered around
outside the house, and got a very strong reaction outside the wall. 'I think your burst pipe's down here. . . .'
I got out a steel punch and a lump hammer, and started

cutting down into the concrete. It took me most of a morning, but when I was about six inches down, the water began to well up through it. Then I reached the earth underneath, and the water began to seep into the hole. I spent the rest of the day enlarging it, suddenly delighted at the prospect of finding the broken pipe, and being able to call in the local plumber to repair it. . . . But although I enlarged the hole to a foot or so, and dug down nearly two feet, I could find no pipe. On the housing estate below us, a bulldozer was in action; I went down and asked him if he could come up and dig through some concrete for me; he agreed to come the next day. By that time Robert had left, to rejoin his family near Penzance. The next morning, the bulldozer arrived. It had a narrow digging shovel with long steel teeth. His method of breaking into the concrete was to pose the shovel, teeth downward, six feet above the ground, then allow it to drop; each time, the teeth bit in deeper. Finally, the surface was cracked enough to tear up the concrete in lumps. I looked on with satisfaction, waiting for the water to spurt from the leak; nothing happened. When he'd reached a depth of six feet, it was obvious that nothing *would* happen. Baffled, I suggested that he dig in another place round the corner— where the water was running in a steady stream from under the house. He tore up the concrete there. No pipe. Finally, I asked him to dig at a spot ten feet away where I *knew* the pipe ran. It was a lucky guess; the pipe made a right-angle bend at that spot, and we could assume that it ran from there straight into the house— several yards from both spots where we'd been tearing up concrete. I cursed Robert, and asked the bulldozer to fill in the holes again. . . . (We solved the water problem by having a new pipe laid from the right-angle bend, around the outside of the house.) When I wrote to him a week later, I mentioned casually that he had been mistaken about the water—but I didn't mention where the pipe was actually situated. He wrote back, commenting that he *had* found another water pipe under the deep freeze, but hadn't bothered to mention it since I seemed so certain the one we were looking for ran outside the house.

So on the whole, I would count our water problem as one of his failures—although, since most of the space under the new room was flooded with water, perhaps this is unfair.

What are my general impressions and conclusions about Robert Leftwich?

I must first state a general principle, which is known to every student of mysticism. 'Strange powers' have nothing to do with what the mystics would call 'knowledge of God.' The Persian mages were, in fact, priests of Zoroaster, and we tend to associate the idea of the 'magician' with *spiritual* power—an idea that has been fostered by the Christian tradition of miracles. According to Sri Ramakrishna, the power to 'work miracles' may be a *by-product* of spiritual advancement; but it is an unimportant by-product. In *The Occult,* I wrote: 'Eusapia Palladino was undoubtedly a genuine medium; yet she was exposed for fraud several times; a kind of genial dishonesty seemed to be part of her character, as of Madame Blavatsky's.' And in my book on Rasputin, I made the same point: that some saints acquire 'power' in the course of spiritual advancement, other men are born with it—like Rasputin, and even Hitler (whose power was, of course, of a different kind)—and may misuse it.

I say this because I am fully aware that if any thoroughgoing sceptic, with a logical-positivist turn of mind, read my account of Leftwich, he would say that it demonstrated nothing but Robert's desire for 'fame,' and my gullibility. In fact, when I first met Robert, I was aware of this possibility. Not that he makes an impression of dishonesty; he doesn't. But that a man so obviously people-oriented might be deceiving himself. On the other hand, his demonstrations with the divining rod made it perfectly clear that he possesses the power of dowsing to a high degree. The more I got to know him, the more I felt that he is basically a solid and consistent character, whose schoolboyish exterior only *seems* to be at variance with the powers he possesses.

I tend to be naturally sympathetic to him because I have always been a rather cheerful and optimistic sort of person, and to some extent, my experience parallels his own. His descriptions of his childhood make it clear that he always had superabundant vitality, and intense curiosity. He mentions that, at the age of five, he used to be up before anyone else in the household—at six a.m.—and out in the street, building dams in the gutter with the aid of a toy sweeping brush. (The odd affinity for water was already apparent.) At school, he developed the knack of concealing his laziness by the trick already mentioned: somehow 'willing' the master to ask him only the questions he knew. The result was that he always did badly in exams; but this was attributed to exam nerves. And in conversations with me, he mentioned several times his lifelong ability to get his own way. (For example, he decided one day that he would like a Kipp's apparatus—a device for producing carbon dioxide in the laboratory. Within a few days, he saw one among a pile of discarded glassware at a factory he was visiting on business; when he asked about the apparatus, the manager said it was going to be thrown out, and told him to take it home. He mentioned a dozen other examples of similar 'coincidences.') He said, wryly, that this ability to get whatever he wants has probably been bad for his character; and, to some extent, this may be true. I am not saying that people need adversity to improve their characters; intelligence and self-criticism will serve just as well; but some problems may turn your attention in a particular direction, and produce important insights. A man with too much power to control his own destiny may be in danger of limiting his experience to what he *thinks* he wants. For example, it may be all very nice to get a Kipp's apparatus within a week of deciding you'd like to own one; but he admits it has been in his attic, unused, ever since.

This breezy, wilful aspect of his character may explain why he is a good 'transmitter' but a poor 'receiver.' He mentioned a friend, Walter Mell, the chief engineer of a large firm, who is a superb receiver. Mell can go out of the room, and Robert thinks of a number, 'transmits' it, and writes it down on a piece of paper. Mell comes into the room, and can announce the four-figure number correctly and without hesitation, before lifting the paper to verify it. But if Robert goes out of the room, and Mell tries to transmit, there is no result. Mell's forehead begins to perspire, and nothing comes into Robert's head. Mell is also a 'sensitive': he can take an object—say, Patricia's watch—and tell her all kinds of things about herself that he cannot possibly have known. Leftwich cannot do this; his mind is attuned to 'doing,' not receiving. Yet when I asked him about this, he remarked, interestingly, that he felt he didn't 'know where to start.' 'Perhaps if I knew where to start, I could do it. But I just don't know.'

This led us on to the subject of dowsing; I asked him

how, in that case, he accounted for his ability to divine almost anything. The answer was important. 'There used to be two schools of thought, and I made a third. One school believes all matter emits some radiation, and some people are sensitive to it. Two, that we emit some minute radar signal that enables us to "pick up" what we're looking for. But this doesn't explain how I can use other people to dowse. I can see a man walking down the street, and tune in to him. And as he passes over, say, a water pipe, he emits a signal which I pick up.' This is obviously not quite accurate; this *is* accounted for by the radar theory. But then, as Leftwich went on to point out, neither of these theories accounts for map dowsing. This is certainly the most baffling form of divining; the map dowser can sit at home, suspend his pendulum—or whatever he uses—over a map, and say: 'There is water in the corner of this field.' Although this sounds preposterous, it is well attested as the more common form of dowsing. In *Rasputin,* I described how a map dowser had taken a letter from me and held it (unopened) in one hand, while he allowed a pendulum to swing above the map of England with the other. The two intersecting lines of its swing pinpointed the place where the sender (Margaret Lane) was at that moment, as I later confirmed. Leftwich believes that *all* dowsing depends on the 'superconscious' mind—a term invented, as far as I know, by Aldous Huxley, who asked why, if the mind has a Freudian 'basement' which is hidden from consciousness, it should not also have a non-Freudian attic.* This, Leftwich believes, is the basic source of the ability to dowse. The superconscious mind is certainly an extremely tempting hypothesis to all who are interested in the theory of

* Introduction to *Human Personality and Its Survival of Bodily Death* by F. W. H. Myers, University Books, New York, 1961.

occultism. It explains, for example, the thousands of well-attested cases of 'spectres of the living.' Goethe relates, for example, how, when he was out for a walk in the rain, he saw a friend wearing his own dressing gown and slippers, walking in front of him. When he arrived home, he found the friend seated in front of the fire in his dressing gown and slippers; he had got soaked on his way to Goethe's house. The friend was completely unaware of having walked in front of Goethe in the rain. And in many cases of 'spectres of the living,' the person whose 'spectre' is seen knows nothing about it —although he may have been thinking about the person to whom it appeared at the time. Telepathy is a possible explanation of these spectres—i.e. the assumption that there was no 'real' spectre, only an *image* of the person in the mind of the 'receiver.' On the other hand, there have been cases in which the spectre has been seen by several people, and it seems unlikely that all are good receivers. Leftwich's 'superconscious' seems a better explanation: that there is a part of the mind whose powers exceed those of normal consciousness, and that can be 'elsewhere'—like Prospero's messenger Ariel—when it pleases. Leftwich has, to some extent, learned the trick of controlling his Ariel.

My own theory of Leftwich's powers is simply this. The superconscious operates efficiently only when our energies are high. It is, in a sense, a 'dispensable' part of the mind, not essential to our survival. Goethe's guest was sitting comfortably in front of the fire, relaxed and thinking about Goethe; perhaps he had a 'peak experience,' one of those spontaneous overflows of sheer joy described by Maslow. The superconscious felt free to go and find Goethe. . . . Most accounts of spectres of the living that I have seen occur either when the person is thinking intently of someone, or is totally relaxed.

Leftwich has always been a person of high energy; consequently, he has always had an active superconscious. The superconscious is, as I have said, the mind's Ariel; sometimes it acts simply as a radar system, warning of danger, possible accidents. ('Accident proneness' and misfortune-proneness in general seem to be connected with low psychic energies, self-pity, tiredness, defeatism.) The superconscious is, basically, the power to *project oneself*. This explains why Leftwich also possesses the power of astral projection, although he is by no means a 'sick sensitive.' (He explained to me that the periods when he can 'project' his astral body are always preceded by a feeling that seems to resemble the feelings of an epileptic before an attack—he has discussed the subject with epileptics in the course of his work for the Samaritans.) It also explains his 'luck,' his ability to get what he wants.

When he came to Cornwall for the first time, he was driving a red sports car. He told me that he always drives very fast—being an impatient sort of person—but he has never had an accident. This, he said, was because his astral body was 'above' the car, enabling him to tell what was coming. I do not think he meant that literally—for when the astral body is being projected, the physical body goes into a trance. He meant, I suspect, that his 'superconscious' enables him to avoid accidents; and he talked about the astral body because he is aware that there is a close connection (perhaps they are even the same thing). He had a typical story about this. One early evening, driving very fast, he was stopped by a police patrol car; an irate policeman asked him if he was aware that he had overtaken dangerously three times within the past five minutes. Robert, with typical precision, explained that he hadn't been overtaking *dangerously*. 'It's difficult to explain, but it's to do with partial detachment from the physical body. The Society for Psychical Research can tell you about it—I'm a member myself.' 'I don't care what bloody society you're a member of. Get out of that bloody car. . . .' But typically, he escaped without a summons, although the patrol car followed him for miles; then, when he thought he'd lost it, another patrol car followed him, obviously alerted by radio to look out for a nut in a red sports car.

The 'superconscious' hypothesis seems to me to explain his rather curious assortment of powers: dowsing, astral projection, 'making things happen' and getting his own way. But it leaves other questions unanswered. For example: are we dealing with 'natural' powers, pure and simple? This was a question also raised in *The Occult*. Primitive people believe in external forces of good and evil; we have gone to the opposite extreme, and try to account for everything in mechanical or natural terms. For example, Lethbridge's theory of ghosts regards them as 'recordings' rather than living creatures. But Robert Leftwich mentioned that there are times when his wife—and other people—feel that he is emanating a force of evil—not strong, perhaps, but noticeable. He says that he is unaware of this; it has nothing to do with malignant thoughts. Is he 'picking it up' from outside himself, and unconsciously transmitting it? I do not know, and he certainly doesn't.

Again, he has the power to stop people smoking. He described the process to me as follows. The subject sits opposite him, and Robert 'attunes' his mind to him. Robert then induces a feeling of numbness in his own fingers. When the subject says, 'My fingers are feeling numb,' he knows the attuning process is complete. At which point he says, 'This is because you're attuned to me. And I can now assure you that you'll never feel the need to smoke again.' This, he says, has been a failure in only one case—and even then, the man gave it up for three years. This sounds closer to telepathy—or straight hypnosis—than to the use of the superconscious. What is the relation between this power of suggestion and the superconscious? Again, I have no idea.

And yet I am strongly inclined to believe that we *are* dealing with natural forces. I have just been playing back the tape I made of a conversation with Leftwich a year ago, and I reflect that Paracelsus would have thought it was sorcery. And so it is, in a way. I know about magnetism imprinting voice patterns in iron oxide; but it still seems strange that a tape should be capable of carrying all the vibrations of the living voice—just as it seems strange to me that a wavy line on the surface of a gramophone record can carry all the complexities of a great orchestra. So it is not difficult to believe that there may be other vibrations and fields of which we are at present ignorant. As I look across the room now, I can see a photograph on the back of a book jacket—a perfectly recognisable face. I pick it up and place it within three inches of my eyes. Now I can see just how little information the page actually carries—just a few blurry patches of black and grey. I hold it at arm's length —again, it is a face. My eyes can obviously 'decode' these patches, and read meaning into them—provided they are given enough of them to form a judgement. As Robert Leftwich walks over the ground, looking for water, some faculty as natural as sight decodes a set of vibrations, and tells him when he has found it. If I take the same dowsing rod, nothing happens; I am, compara- tively speaking, 'short sighted.'

But amid all my uncertainties, I am fairly sure of one thing. Robert Leftwich is a non-passive personality; in fact, he is a highly active personality, whose psyche has always exerted a definite pressure on the outside world, in the form of curiosity, expectancy, interest. Such pressure is like water; it finds its way into cracks, and enlarges them. His powers are the outcome of his *attitude*. He demonstrates, to my satisfaction, that psychic powers are a matter of choice, not of chance.

CHAPTER TWO

Mrs. Eunice Beattie

As an 'occult investigator,' I am aware that I'm thoroughly unsatisfactory. When I ought to be asking penetrating questions, or devising means of testing the truth of what I am being told, I simply listen and make notes. This, I suspect, is because I see the world through the eyes of a novelist. In a sense, I am incurious about people—about their affairs, their lives; but I'm interested in the way their minds work, in their motivations. From a fairly early age, I developed the conviction that most people waste their lives because they see the world falsely. Anyone can understand what is meant if we say that someone is 'utterly conventional': that such a person accepts a set of social values without question, like a sheep that never feels curious about what lies on the other side of the hedge. But we find it altogether more difficult to grasp that we all live according to a set of conventions of *consciousness:* that, on the whole, we see and hear what we expect to see and hear, and that there may be enormous areas of experience that cannot get past our mental filters. For example, can you imagine Mr. Pickwick appreciating the music of Beethoven, or the painting of Goya? (Can you imagine Dickens himself appreciating it, if it comes to that?) Could Jane Austen, even with the greatest stretch of the imagination, understand the murders committed by the Charles Manson 'family'? Our perceptions have certain inbuilt limitations; yet, in a sense, it is *we* who limit them, as we might turn down the volume control on the radio to what we consider a 'bearable volume.' This is why Rimbaud dreamed of an 'ordered derangement of the senses,' deliberately pushing the senses beyond their normal limits.

This is why I would find Robert Leftwich an interesting character, even if I cannot state positively that all his claims are true and unexaggerated. He is aware that the normal boundaries are not absolutes; he wants to break out beyond them. Like Rimbaud, he has already rejected the 'communal life-world.' A world in which there were millions of people like him would be, for me, a more interesting place.

And the same applies to Mrs. Eunice Beattie, who is otherwise about as unlike Leftwich as could be imagined. Outwardly she appears to be a perfectly ordinary person—a retired nurse, devoted to her married son and his family, living in an attractive suburb of Plymouth. She has written (and typed) hundreds of pages that reveal that either (a) she has a remarkable mind, or (b) that she has 'tuned in' to other intelligences and transcribed some of their ideas.

I have not kept a record of when I first met Mrs. Beattie, but it must have been in the early months of 1972. It was at the time when I was still receiving floods of correspondence about *The Occult,* which had appeared the previous autumn. Mrs. Beattie's letter said that she hoped I wouldn't consider her a crank, but that she had been producing automatic writing that seemed to her to answer some basic questions about human purpose and destiny. I replied that I'd like to see some of it, and asked her if she would like to come and have

lunch at the Westward TV studios next time I was there.
I gave her the date.

I'd forgotten about her when a message came to say
that a lady wanted to see me at the desk. I went down,
and found Mrs. Beattie looking nervously out of the
window, as if tempted to dash out into the street. I
asked her to come into the canteen for lunch. As soon
as we sat down, she handed me a manilla folder full of
manuscript. I opened it, and saw that the first page was
headed with a quotation from one of Arthur Waley's
translations of a Chinese poem. I read it with a certain
amount of pleasure—an understandable reaction, I
think, when one is faced with a great sheaf of original
manuscript that may be totally unreadable. It is like
finding an oasis in a desert. I asked her if she liked
Chinese poetry. She looked blank; then, when I pointed
to the Waley quotation, said she had no idea who
Arthur Waley was. It had simply been 'dictated' to her.
I glanced at the rest of the typescript, and saw mentions
of Walt Whitman and Angelus Silesius. 'What about
these? Have you read them?' 'No. Who is Walt Whitman?'

As we ate, I looked at her curiously. She seemed shy,
rather tense, as if trying to cut herself off from the
sounds of the room. She was small, attractive, around
sixty; a journalist might take the easy way out and describe her as motherly, but the rather smart hair style
and the neat clothes reminded me that she had been a
hospital sister—she had told me that in her letter. Very
much the type children take to—as I discovered when
she met my children. She didn't strike me as in any way
a crank; or, for that matter, anything like my idea of a
'psychic': neither the professional spirit medium, nor the
visionary peasant woman of the type described by Yeats.
I found her very difficult to place.

She came and watched the programme being video-taped, sitting quietly in a corner of the studio without speaking to anybody. Afterwards I asked her if she'd found it interesting. 'Oh, yes. Fascinating.' But I had a feeling she wouldn't have said so unless I'd asked her.

Clearly, I wasn't going to be able to assess her without seeing rather more of her. I asked her if she could come to my home that weekend. She looked anxious. 'Are you sure your wife won't object?' 'I don't think so.' 'Perhaps you'd better ask her first and let me know.'

Before we left the studio, I asked her how she had come to write me. I expected her to say that she'd read something about *The Occult,* or seen me on television. Again she surprised me. 'Your name came floating into my head one day. I'd no idea who you were. Then, a week later, I saw something about you in a newspaper. I had an odd feeling that I ought to get in touch with you.'

When I told Joy I'd asked Mrs. Beattie over for the weekend, she asked, 'What sort of a person is she?' and I had to admit I didn't know. I could only say she seemed a perfectly ordinary, normal person and I didn't think she'd be a difficult guest. Apart from Robert Leftwich, my acquaintance with 'psychics' had been small. In my early twenties, when I was working at United Dairies, Chiswick, I had met a woman called Grace who worked in the canteen (I have forgotten her other name), and I had been convinced that she possessed unusual powers. She seemed to be an ordinary, middle-aged cockney lady, of the kind you'd find behind almost any counter in any works canteen in the country; but Joy and I spent an evening with her, and I realised that she 'knew' a great deal—in the sense that Gurdjieff did; and the things she was able to tell me about myself startled me. Mrs. Beattie seemed as ordinary as Grace; and I was

willing to give her the benefit of the doubt. I am aver-
agely sceptical, and I was aware of the possibility that
she might be suffering from delusions, or might be making it all up to make herself interesting. I didn't believe
for a moment that she was suffering from delusions.
Neither did it seem likely that she was making it all up—
although I had to entertain the possibility. She was a
widow, living on her own—and, by her own admission,
without many close friends. I settled down to reading her
manuscript, hoping it might provide clues. And the first
thing that was obvious was that *if* she was pulling my
leg, then it wasn't a recently conceived plan. She'd written a lot, and over a long period; there were diary references dating back ten years. And it soon struck me, from
the general tone of her writing, that she is deeply and
genuinely preoccupied with what we loosely term 'the
spiritual.' Now when some average, not-very-intelligent
person becomes obsessed with religion, the result is an
obvious feeling of unbalance; their minds become lop-
sided; they spout the jargon, but it is almost a meaningless noise. In fact, it becomes a kind of mask, designed to
hide their stupidity. The most obvious thing about Mrs.
Beattie's writing was that it was carefully and painstak-
ingly saying something, and what it was saying was close
to what all saints and mystics have always said. 'We are
completely dependent on the creative energy of God,
from our first breath. Our lives are usually wrecked by
our sense of personal power.' Aldous Huxley's anthology
of mysticism, *The Perennial Philosophy,* is full of these
statements about the need to abandon the 'Self,' to become identified with the Not-Self. 'There are many,' said
Mrs. Beattie, 'who are branches of a tree that are cut off
from the main stem, and who do not know they are
dying.' I got a feeling she knew what she was talking
about; this was not just religious gobbledegook. And

there were places where I suddenly found myself reading with increased interest. 'Man in his spiritual state is both male and female, and can thus create for himself—just as his Father can. Christ said that all he could do, men could do also, when they had come to full realisation.' For some months before meeting Mrs. Beattie, I had been struggling with the obscure but impressive work of a Hungarian philosopher, Charlotte Bach, whose studies of sexual perversion—particularly of 'trans-sexuality' (i.e. the man's desire to become a woman, and vice versa) had led her to a completely new theory of evolution, in which the inner tensions created by this sexual ambiguity drive man up the evolutionary ladder. She had also noted that some human beings achieve a precarious balance through the creative act. Mrs. Beattie seemed to be stating the same thing much more simply. In many ways, she might be poles apart from the formidably intellectual and erudite Mrs. Bach; but she seemed equally aware of the possibilities of an evolution of consciousness. A disciple of Gurdjieff's once said that his system was 'a method of preventing your past from becoming your future'; the same preoccupation ran throughout these manuscripts of Mrs. Beattie's.

Now if that was all there was to it, I would have no difficulty about placing Mrs. Beattie. I would say that she was one of my 'outsiders, driven by deeper urges than most people, and therefore feeling rather out of place in our ordinary, working society. That in spite of this, in spite of a lack of formal education, she had gradually taught herself to think for herself, and achieved some degree of insight into the problem of the evolution of spiritual consciousness.'

But her writing made it clear that it was more complicated than that. After some study, it seemed to me that there were three distinct aspects to Mrs. Beattie. To begin with, there was the straight religious aspect: the pre-occupation with what most religious people would call salvation, and which she is inclined to call evolution. Next, there was the occultist strain, which might be reminiscent of the work of Emanuel Swedenborg:

'I went out of my body one night, in the usual way, but instead of determining my destination, I was called instead; I found that I was on a high plateau, up in a mountainous country; it was very beautiful. There were a group of people, all dressed in white. One of these was my teacher, and he came to me, and said that this night, they were going to show me some scenes from the history of the world. I sat down among them, and then picture after picture came before me, and I sat and watched as I saw the world as it used to be. They told me I was looking at scenes in the race memory.'

And this was closely connected to another aspect: pre-vision or prophecy. Some of these sound more like Nostradamus than Swedenborg: 'The coast of France will change overnight. Paris will fall to rocket bombardment.' 'One man shall govern the world, centuries ahead; far, too far ahead for us to see.' 'A rain of meteors on the earth; I think it is a periodic cycle.' She also predicts that Rome will become a heap of ashes (this may be connected to another prophecy to the effect that the Roman Catholic Church—and all others—will fail), and that the last Pope will be called Peter. She says that there is now a child in Asia, about ten years old, who will govern all the east. 'A more evil man has never been born.' New York will be shaken by a great earthquake. 'This will be caused by the rising of the east coast out of the water; this will cause a tidal wave, and Ireland will be covered by water.' (Edgar Cayce, the American healer and prophet, made similar predictions about the east coast of America.) The Chinese will conquer Europe as far as Scandinavia and most of the populations of Italy and Austria will be wiped out by aerial weapons.

Another entry reads: 'May 1969: A new planet will be discovered at the end of 1970—there may be another one later on. Nov. 1971: This was verified on TV last week.' A later entry clarifies this: '3 Jan. 73: Outer planet, Poseidon, confirmed as belonging to our system. Theory of explosion within our system confirmed, as theory of our scientists to explain odd orbit of Poseidon and last two planets.'

From my point of view, the 'religious' parts of her writing were the least interesting. 'Each man must follow his own path to God, and there is no one way. Only his own personal way—and this Christ will teach him when he opens his mind and heart to him.' True, no doubt, but it could have been written by anybody.

Altogether more interesting was the description of direct experience scattered among the pages. This, for example:

'I, too, was once the same; I did not believe anything but the evidence of my own senses. Yet something pulled at my heart, and I was not happy. I longed to believe in something or someone; I also wanted to know why the universe was, why men were, and what for, and why we were born, and died, and where did we go when we died? . . . There was a reason, I knew there must be. No one would go to the trouble of creating a universe for no reason. So I tried to reach this Person by talking to Him. I spoke in my own way, being essentially a simple and direct person. . . . I told this Person what was troubling me, I said I wanted to know, and was willing to learn, and I would work hard to understand, if He would tell me. He said: "First, you must be tried. . . ." He told me to meet Him every day at the same hour. This I did most faithfully, and little by little, He taught me and trained me, until I reached the point where I cannot learn more until I pass over into the soul world.' She adds that 'He' speaks into the mind, like a silent whisper, which has the effect of filling her with joy.

In another place, she describes how she was taught astral projection. 'I was to rest flat upon either a bed, divan or floor, supported by a pillow—if necessary covered by a quilt. Then to begin recollection—this was in the early days. Later I relaxed through habit and began meditation immediately: first step: concentration upon mind, relax the body; it becomes still and heavy. Second step: the mind slowly begins to become quiet, the breathing slows. Concentration into the direct centre of conscious mind—it stills and smooths out. Concentration has forgotten body, and is entirely closed into the centre of mind. The mind stills, and becomes smooth as a still pond, then stops. This is the point where one looks into a silence, or darkness . . . yet it is not darkness, but a light so intense as to blind one, and one sees darkness. There one is poised and utterly still, intense concentration, and listening intensely. And one waits and waits and waits. Sometimes there is nothing but an answering warmth. Sometimes a voice speaks and one *sees* exactly what is said. If one is needed for a lesson, or some other reason, this is the point where I leave the body. First there is a short blank, and then I am fully conscious beside my body. At first the second body was nude, but I was taught to will it clothed. Occasionally, I would pass other souls who were unconscious, and at times beginners who were not clothed, but answering a summons—one can always tell.'

Well, all this was fairly plain, and what I now needed was to talk further with Mrs. Beattie to clarify and enlarge. I met her off the train at St. Austell on a Friday evening. On the journey home, she talked about her son

John, his wife and children, and various other practical matters; she seemed to have no inclination to talk about her writing. But she confirmed that much of it was 'automatic': that she felt a sudden impulse to sit down and begin to write; her hand twitched, and as soon as she seized a pen, it began writing.

Back home, she met Joy and my three children. The youngest, then less than a year old, wasn't much interested in strangers, but the other two—age six and eleven —took to her immediately. My six-year-old son Damon seemed to accept her as a kind of extra grandmother, and lost no time in climbing on her and demanding stories. Obviously, as far as the children were concerned, her 'vibrations' were good. Sally, who had overheard me telling Joy about Mrs. Beattie's feats of astral projection, immediately began asking her questions about it. Mrs. Beattie answered factually, without evasion or embarrassment. I got the feeling that Sally thought it was all a bit weird, but not 'scary.' As the daughter of a writer, she gets used to meeting all kinds of people.

There is not much to tell about that weekend. I didn't want to ask lots of questions unless she obviously wanted to talk; and as she seemed quite contented to play with the children and talk to Joy, I didn't press it. It was just a matter of getting to know her, and letting things happen. She didn't seem to have any faddist preferences. She ate meat, and when we took her to the local pub on Saturday evening, she drank Moselle wine with me. There was only one odd event. As she was sitting opposite me, on the settee, her right hand began to jump about, rather in the way your leg twitches if a doctor strikes the knee to test your reflexes. Pointing to it with her other hand, she said: 'Look, someone's trying to get through.' 'Who?' 'I don't know. That's how it usually happens.' She went on talking, and the hand continued to twitch. At this point, Sally, who was watching it with interest, got a pencil and notepad, and asked her to see what 'they' wanted. She took the pencil, and began to scribble, in an odd, jerky way. After thirty seconds or so, she read it, wrinkled her nose, and handed it to me. It certainly didn't seem to make sense. 'Hearken unto me,' repeated three times, and then some such message as 'I am that which is eternal.' (Unfortunately, although we kept the paper, it has got mislaid.) The 'Hearken unto me' made it sound like some religious crank with a desire to be heard, but nothing much to say. I asked her: 'Do you often get messages like that?' She shrugged. 'Sometimes. Sometimes it doesn't make sense.' Over the next few minutes, as she talked, her hand twitched periodically, but she ignored it, as if it was a telephone she didn't want to answer. . . . Which led me to reflect that the 'spirit world' obviously has its nuts and cranks too, its persistent talkers who are convinced they have something of world-shattering significance to communicate, when all they really want is attention. An interesting thought—that perhaps even disembodied spirits may be unfulfilled neurotics. . . . Or is it possible that some of these voices are from Mrs. Beattie's subconscious? I suspect she would say no, for the subconscious mind plays a definite part in her system of ideas. . . . I have always been fascinated by the way the subconscious can throw up ideas and images that seem totally independent of the conscious personality. For example, on the edge of sleep, the images and thoughts that wash through the mind seem to be as objective as the sea, coming from *somewhere else*, not from your own memory banks. . . .

When I drove Mrs. Beattie to the station on the following Monday morning, I still hadn't made up my mind about her. It would have been all very straightforward if she had been one of Yeats's simple, illiterate peasant women; then there would be no doubt that everything she wrote came from somewhere outside her own conscious mind. But she struck me as a fairly acute and astute person, and in much of her writing, she speaks with a direct personal voice—as in the passages quoted above. If *these* are not 'automatic writing,' then where does the personal writing end and the 'dictated writing' begin?

At which point, it is necessary to make some general comments on 'automatic writing.' And the first thing that must be said flatly is that *no* spirit message, whether received via a medium, automatic script, or even on recorded tape (as in Constantin Raudive's experiments) has ever said anything of profound importance. As far as I know, there is no automatic script on record that says anything that the actual writer (i.e. the person holding the pencil) would not have been capable of saying. The London housewife Mrs. Rosemary Brown has produced many piano works which she believes are dictated by dead composers such as Chopin, Schumann, Liszt, and it seems to me highly unlikely that she is a fraud.* On the other hand, she has not produced a single piece that can be seriously compared with the best of these composers. If she could produce a piece of Chopin or Liszt as popular as the 'Minute Waltz' or 'Liebestraum' she would convert thousands of sceptics. She is now apparently engaged in taking down Beethoven's Tenth Symphony from the composer's dictation; an exciting prospect—but experience tells me that it will be a noisy, pretentious piece with a few echoes of the Fifth and Ninth symphonies.

In *Modern Spiritualism* (1902), Frank Podmore (one

* See *The Occult*, pp. 496–8.

of the founders of the SPR) has several chapters on automatic writing, trance utterance, and so on. Mrs. Cora Tappan of America could produce an incredible flow of words, both in prose and verse, and it usually 'made sense'; but the extracts Podmore quotes never rise above the inspiration, say, of *Hymns Ancient and Modern*. A spirit who professed to be Francis Bacon asked whether 'in the whole history of written thought there is anything that can approach [his trance utterances] in the magnitude of the ideas or the profundity of the thoughts,' and a believer named Tallmadge admitted that 'their equal never proceeded from mortal man.' A glance at some examples of 'Bacon's' eloquence and profundity is a let-down:

'How glorious that man's destiny! He leaves behind the errors of time, and boldly pushing forward through the untried future, he plants his standard on the very outward wall of eternity, and here he makes his stand. . . .'

And so on and so on, with the clichés clashing like cymbals. The spirits give no evidence whatever of the kind of *sharpness* of mind that we associate with genius. It is all woolly and bombastic. One single cutting verse by the spirit of Heine would carry more conviction than reams of pseudo-Bacon. In my own opinion, it requires a certain degree of self-deception to see anything very remarkable in most 'spirit teachings' or messages from the dead. I can think of only one occasion when the results were well above the usual standard: in that curious automatic script that W. B. Yeats published under the title of *A Vision*. With its complicated explanation of how different types of human character correspond to different phases of the moon, this is a work of considerable fascination. Yeats's biographers generally accept his story that his wife Georgie wrote down most of the book at the dictation of 'spirits'; the fact remains that it *is* the kind of thing Yeats might have written as an exercise in cosmological speculation, and there is not a word in it that Yeats could not have written.

Am I suggesting that all automatic writing is fraud? Not for a moment. It *is* possible that only the subconscious mind is involved—or perhaps the 'superconscious' that Robert Leftwich speaks of. But in that case, it would be reasonable to suppose that all so-called 'spirit phenomena' are purely subjective—springing from unseen depths of the human mind—and the evidence is against that. On the whole, the weight of evidence suggests that communication with the dead explains various spirit messages at least as well as the hypothesis of fraud or telepathy. (I have discussed this at length in *The Occult*.) So automatic writing finds itself in an embarrassing kind of limbo: never totally convincing, but much too convincing to be dismissed as fraud or self-deception. In *most* spirit writing (or painting, or, in the case of Rosemary Brown, music) the evidence is on the side of subconscious mental activity. For example, a great deal of 'spirit painting' has more merit—and talent —than the painter is able to call upon when painting normally and consciously; but in view of our tendency to under-utilise our powers (discussed earlier), this is what we might expect.

So when I settled down to studying Mrs. Beattie's manuscripts, I had no expectation of discovering profound revelations. And I didn't find any. But there *were* a great many keen insights, some of them exciting: 'When Roger Bannister ran the four minute mile, he made it possible for all men to do it. Since that time, many have done so—the potential for this had always been there, but no one else had tried it; the time had not yet come. So it is with all things, in the way of evolution.' That struck me as way above the level of the eloquence and profundity of 'Francis Bacon.' It is an oddity that has been observed by writers on mountaineering. First a mountain is regarded as unclimbable; men die in the attempt. Then someone succeeds; and within a couple of decades, Sunday school teachers are taking parties of children up it.

On the other hand, there were misunderstandings. 'Ouspensky says: "The soul and the future life are one and the same." It is imperative to keep our souls, if we are to win eternal life. . . .' But Ouspensky was saying something much profounder than that. He meant that man is a fragmented creature with thousands of 'I's,' all replacing one another minute by minute. How can such a creature have a 'future'? His future is shared out between a thousand selves. In the same way, how can he be said to have a soul? He has a thousand fragments of soul, like a shattered mirror. So to achieve unity (a single 'self' or soul) would also entail having a real future.

On the other hand, the spirit generally pervading the manuscript is close to that of Ramakrishna, the Hindu saint who went into a state of *samadhi* (ecstasy) at the mere mention of the name 'God' or 'Krishna.' 'Tell yourself that God is good, unchangeably good. That He exists in you, and that without Him you could not exist at all. Feel a desire to unite with Him, so that He may express Himself through you. Feel God as love.' The words are trite, but the overall impression is of a genuine, deep, strong religious impulse, not of someone repeating religious platitudes. There is a strong overall feeling of genuineness. The insights are real: for example, the recognition that most human beings are hopelessly passive, failing to recognise that 'all power comes from within,' and that 'we are weak only when we fail to recognise this.' This is, of course, the same basic recognition as in Robert Leftwich's book. And once I had noted this similarity, I noted many others: the insistence on the importance of discipline and responsibility, for example. She writes of the necessities for spiritual evolution: to lead an ordered life, to keep the body as fit as possible, and not to 'use it to excess,' to accept obligations to family and society, and take up a profession according to our capacities. No outsider-ish 'opting out,' no

> Do what you will, this world's a fiction
> And is made up of contradiction . . .

Again, she agrees with Leftwich that it is necessary to 'retire' in order to be able to devote time to thinking and self-knowledge. 'Since retirement I live a secluded life, a kind of contemplative life. It would not be possible to live the normal everyday working life full-time and to be able to have this kind of inner-experience. This is not possible; which is why, I think, I was able to leave the body only before and after I had ceased to live a full emotional sex life and a full-time working life. All levels of consciousness, as well as the 3 bodies, have to be in alignment, in harmony, at rest, before real contemplative experience is possible.' Passages like this have a definite sense of authenticity.

Certain phrases—like the reference to the three bodies—puzzled me. When I asked Mrs. Beattie about them, she would refer me back to the manuscript, saying they were explained there; but I couldn't see them, or the explanations were mixed up with other matters, which confused me. So the next time she came over for a weekend, I asked her to sit down and talk into a tape recorder, giving me details of her life, and an outline of her basic ideas.

Eunice Battie was born in Bangor, North Wales, and grew up on a nearby farm—which had been in her family for generations. (I was surprised to realise she was Welsh—she has no trace of the accent.) It was interesting to realise she was a Celt. There was a tradition in her family (although she admits she is not sure whether there is any truth in it) that one member of each generation should become a hermit, and a kind of priest. The 'religion,' as she described it, sounded like some curious survival of paganism; the family would go to some kind of stone circle near the farm, and perform a harvest festival type of ceremony that involved placing wheat, honey and water on a flat stone which served as an altar. (Note that the harvest festival, as known in English churches today, was introduced in the nineteenth century by the Rev. R. S. Hawker, the poet and smuggler of Morwenstow.) A prayer was offered in Welsh. And just before Christmas, the family decorated a cauldron, known as Ceridwen's cauldron, with holly. This sounds like the kind of semi-pagan survival described by Margaret Murray, although Mrs. Beattie insists that it was a simple religious ceremony, nothing to do with witchcraft.

Her childhood was completely normal—attending school, working on the farm (with her brothers and sisters). She was always lonely, and regarded by the rest of the family as delicate, although she only suffered the usual childish illnesses. It was at sixteen that she had her first unusual experience. One night, just before dawn, she woke up and found herself standing beside her bed, and looking down on her body which lay in the bed. There was a man standing beside her—or rather a figure, whose body seemed to be an area of luminosity. She could only see his head, although this was not particularly clear. This 'man' she refers to as her teacher. He told her that he had brought her out of her body, and that he wanted to warn her that she would have a serious accident within two weeks. Precisely fourteen days later, the brakes on her bicycle failed and she was thrown into a brick wall; she spent several weeks in hospital. I wondered why her teacher couldn't simply have warned her to have her brakes looked at by the local repairman, but she went on a moment later to say that the accident, and the period in hospital, were essential to her evolution. This is an interesting point. Many 'psychics' have started their careers with an accident or serious illness. (In *The Occult,* I have cited the well-authenticated case of Peter Hurkos, who became psychic after receiving a serious head injury when he fell off a ladder; when he woke up in hospital, he found he could read people's thoughts and 'see' their future.)

Subsequently, she had many experiences of astral projection. At this point, she explained the puzzling business of the 'three bodies.' There is, apart from the physical body, an electromagnetic (or energy) body, and the 'astral' body (which she prefers to call the emotional or soul-body). The energy body would seem to be what Harold Burr measures with his voltmeters, and what the Kirlian device detects. The astral body is the body that travels—perhaps Robert Leftwich's superconscious. The energy body hovers above the physical body when it is unconscious—or anaesthetised. Mrs. Beattie said she had often seen this in the operating theatre. (The psychic Phoebe Payne, quoted in *The Occult,* was also able to see the 'auras' of flowers and animals. The inference would seem to be that people like Mrs. Beattie and Phoebe Payne have a sense that can detect the 'energy body' like the Kirlian device.) The aura, in a healthy person, spreads out about a foot beyond the physical body, and it radiates various colours—depending on the consciousness of the individual. When the individual is tired, the aura dims.

She laid a great deal of stress on this matter of vital energy. I found it interesting because I had recently been fascinated by an account of experiments carried out at McGill University, as described in Lyall Watson's important book *Supernature*. Barley seeds were treated with salt and baked in an oven—but not long enough to kill them. They were then planted, and some were treated with water which had been held for thirty minutes per day by a known 'healer.' The plants treated with this water gave appreciably better results than those treated with ordinary tap water. Moreover, when the water was 'treated' by a woman suffering from severe depression and a man with psychotic tendencies, the growth of the seeds was notably retarded. These experiments by Bernard Grad, which seem to confirm the findings of Harold Burr, also fit the pattern of Mrs. Beattie's own insights into the subject of vital energy. (Oddly enough, chemical analysis of the water treated by 'healers' revealed a slight spreading between the hydrogen and oxygen atoms.)

This led Mrs. Beattie to make some comments on negative people and 'vampirism'—the way that some people can drain your energy, so you feel completely worn out after half an hour with them. It was a phenomenon, she said, that she had often noted when working on old people's wards. They would get into a thoroughly negative state of mind, and drain the energy of anyone who worked on the ward. I asked her whether the negative attitude causes their sickness, or vice versa. I could guess what her answer would be, and I was right: that most sickness is caused by 'negativity,' and begins with the energy body, which then affects the physical body. 'The mind affects the emotions, the emotions affect the energy, the energy affects the physical body.'

The effect of her accident at sixteen was to give her certain powers of insight, of the same type as Peter Hurkos'. She found that she often knew about people simply by looking at them, and found that by looking at their hands—or the tea leaves left in their cups—she was able to describe their lives and foretell the future. This was 'instinctive,' she said—and it sounds, as she describes it, not unlike Robert Leftwich's description of dowsing. At a later stage, these powers diminished, although they never faded.

She had no definite idea of what she wanted to do when she grew up—only that she didn't want to marry a farmer and settle down to existence as a housewife. When she thought about it, she was inclined to feel that she would become a nurse or a nun. But by the time she left school, her father had left the farm and moved to Knowsley, near Liverpool, where he took over a market garden on Lord Derby's estate. Eunice worked for her father—tending greenhouses, wrapping flowers. From the family's point of view the change was a success; her father proved to be a good market gardener, and the business prospered. From Eunice's point of view, it was less satisfactory; after farm life in Wales, she found the English too practical and down to earth. It was lucky that she could work for her father. The out-of-the-body experiences continued to happen periodically, preceded by a feeling of introspection, a desire to 'sink into herself.' She told no one of these experiences. She also decided, at a fairly early stage, that it was important to keep these experiences secret; she felt that this was essential if she was to live a normal life.

At the age of 22½, she was ready to leave home; she wanted to get as far away as possible. So she answered an advertisement to become a nurse—a probationer—at a hospital at Kingston on Thames. At that time, hospital work was a vocation rather than a career. Pay was minimal; they had to work long hours, and buy their own uniforms. But it was about the only vocation—apart from a nunnery—that suited her temperament. The problem, as always, was simply the amount of work involved; she would be so exhausted at the end of a day that there was no time for spiritual adventures.

As she described all this to me, I found myself forming a definite picture of what was involved, and realising that, in a way, it was not so very different from my own teens and early twenties—or, for that matter, of anybody who has this romantic impulse to escape from the world. Thomas Mann's novel *Buddenbrooks* contains a classic portrait of the 'artist as a young man,' and the chapter on Hanno's visits to the seaside—as a child—is particularly powerful: the sense of release, the peace, the delight, the freedom, of wide beaches, seaweed on the rocks, anemones in pools, hours of lying quietly on the sand, 'while you let your eyes rove idly and lose themselves in the green and blue infinity beyond. There was the air that swept in from that infinity—strong, free, wild, gently sighing and deliciously scented; it seemed to enfold you round, to veil your hearing and make you pleasantly giddy, and blessedly submerge all consciousness of time and space.' And I can recall, at fifteen or sixteen, spending evenings reading poetry in my bedroom, while all the tensions gradually relaxed out of the soul, until you felt tired, but completely serene and free, like someone who is convalescing from a dangerous illness. Thomas Mann felt that this capacity for total relaxation, the longing for 'dim hills and far horizons,' makes one unfit for normal life; it is almost inevitable that Hanno should die young. Mrs. Beattie has always

been made of stronger stuff; she has always been prepared to live a normal life and work for a living. . . .

What I am now suggesting—with no certainty of being on the right track—is that the forces that were
struggling to find an outlet in her were very much the
same forces that produce all literature and art. They seek
out whatever channels are available to them. Yeats's imagination turned to fairy lands and the world of the occult. A young Cornishman named Leslie Rowse—from
a working-class background—managed to win a scholar-
ship to Oxford, and become a historian, finding in the
study of the past the same release that Yeats found in
his fairy lands. Einstein found the same release in the
world of stars and atoms; Freud in the dark waters of
the unconscious. But poets and artists and scientists
have a path to follow; once they have seen it, all they
have to do is stick to it. A girl brought up to feed
chickens and tend flowers had no comparable outlet;
the creative energies turned inward. A Freudian would
talk about 'compensations,' even of sexual unfulfil-
ment, and there I think he would be wrong. Mrs. Beattie said wryly that she always thought of herself as an old
maid; but she admitted that, as a teenager, and as a
nurse, she had flirtations and occasionally went out with
boys. She would be unlikely to meet anyone like herself
in the hospital milieu; so the lack of interest in sex was
basically a failure to find anyone who appealed to her
as an ideal.

In fact, she did marry eventually. During the war—
by which time she was working as a district nurse in
Liverpool—she met an RAF man in a bus queue just
as the sirens were sounding for an air raid; they got into
conversation; he saw her home, and eventually, they
married. Marriage didn't suit her; it was not what she
was looking for. Almost immediately she felt she had

done the wrong thing, and her inner life marked time. In 1947, her son John was born. Some two years later, her husband, who had taken a job with the Ministry of Supply, was killed when he was taking a car out on test. 'It was an emotional shock, but I suppose it was a kind of relief as well.' I don't think the comment indicates heartlessness. Her life so far had given her few opportunities for self-expression, self-development— what Maslow would call self-actualisation. Work as a nurse was far from ideal, long hours of patrolling wards, changing sheets, emptying bedpans; and being a district nurse, while it was more interesting, was also nonstop hard work. She tried marriage and realised it was another cul-de-sac, as far as self-actualisation was concerned (although she was a doting mother).

From the practical point of view, the death of her husband meant loss of security. She had been working in a hospital (Bootle Maternity) during her marriage; now she decided to become a district nurse again. When John was ten, she decided to widen her field to social work, specialising in children. This was the most rewarding work she had done so far. John was at school in a religious community in Shropshire; she enjoyed social work, and the variety of people it brought her into contact with. The same insight that had enabled her to tell fortunes now made her a good social worker. Finally, she moved to Plymouth—to Freedom Fields Hospital—and became a sister in the maternity unit. She was there until her retirement three years ago. And now, after forty years, she at last had the freedom to pursue her 'habit' (as she once called it): that capacity to retire deep into herself, achieve a state of inner serenity, and then leave the body. At no stage has she regarded herself as a 'psychic' or potential medium; the evolutionary preoccupation has always been there. These 'astral' activities were strictly for the purpose of self-actualisation. Her view was confirmed in discussion with Father Trevor Huddleston, who agreed that too much preoccupation with the 'psychic' could place an obstacle in the way of spiritual progress.

By this time, the sceptically inclined reader will be asking why I should believe a single word she told me, since she offered no 'proof' of any unusual power. And I can only say: Because most of what she said 'fitted in' to things I already knew or suspected. I was groping my way towards some general theory of 'hidden powers' and astral projection, trying to relate them back to known psychological facts.

My basic assumption is that we possess ranges of power that we do not suspect. Anybody who has ever bought some gadget—like a tape recorder—knows that it is necessary to read the handbook before you can fully understand all the things you can do with it. If you don't read the handbook, you may have it for years without realising that a certain button will enable you to superimpose one recording on another, or that a socket is intended for an earphone that automatically cuts out the main loudspeaker. . . . Human beings come without instruction books, and we have to find out our potentialities by trial and error. And since most of us lack the exploratory urge, we never discover all our capacities. To take a simple example: most of us can wake up at a certain definite hour if we have to, as if we possessed some inner alarm clock; but, as far as I know, no psychologist has ever concluded an investigation into this 'power,' to find out how it works. Again, we have all experienced 'second wind,' the ability to call upon vital reserves; but no one knows *where* these vital reserves are stored.

Now, the power to 'retreat within oneself' is one of our

most interesting human capacities. I do not mean simply to go off into a daydream; most daydreaming is a negative thing, a kind of inattention, a 'switching off,' a form of loss of memory. On the other hand, a child sometimes becomes so completely absorbed in a book that it is just as if he has retreated to a room inside himself. You can often see it in a young mother breast-feeding a baby; it is as if she and the baby had retreated into an inner-room. In *Wolf Solent*, John Cowper Powys described Wolf's 'trick of sinking into his soul,' which Wolf calls his 'mythology.' Powys describes it as 'a device that supplied him with the secret substratum of his whole life.'

'This "sinking into his soul" . . . consisted of a certain summing-up, to the surface of his mind, of a subconscious magnetic power which . . . as he watched the glitter of sun and moon upon the waters from that bow window, had seemed to prepare to answer such a summons.'

In the later novel *Porius*, Powys invents yet another word for this ability, 'cavoseniargising,' which he describes:

'. . . those recurrent moments in his life when the gulf between the animal consciousness of his body . . . and the consciousness of his restless soul was temporarily bridged; so that his soul found itself to follow every curve and ripple of his bodily sensations, *and yet remain suspended above them* . . .' (*Porius*, p. 83).

This process of self-withdrawal is undoubtedly one of the major unexplored secrets of human nature. And the discovery of psychedelic drugs in the late forties suggested some interesting new methods of exploration. Aldous Huxley was the first to assert, in his two books on the mescalin experience, that man's 'inner landscapes' could be as vast and as varied as the surface of the earth. Since then, there have been many attempts to chart this inner world. One of the most interesting—because the most reasonable and logical—is *The Centre of the Cyclone,* by John Lilly. Dr. Lilly is a scientist, whose early work on the mind of the dolphin attracted considerable attention. Later on, he experimented with sensory deprivation in a tank of lukewarm water, and experienced dreamlike states, trancelike states, mystical states. It was during the course of these experiments that he began to have experiences which could have been delusions, but which seemed to have a certain authenticity: a feeling of apparently being joined by other people in the dark, floating environment, and times when he 'apparently tuned in on networks of communication that are normally below our levels of awareness, networks of civilisations way beyond ours.' He decided to try the effect of LSD—lysergic acid—in the water-tank. He describes how, in this first experiment, there was a sense of completely black, completely silent, empty space without a body. He called it the 'zero point,' and says: 'I wish to emphasise that this zero point was not in the body, it was out in the universe of nothing except silence and blackness. . . .' A positivist would say this is just quibbling with words; he was still 'in his body,' even if his imagination produced a sensation of outer space. The positivist could be right; but I am not sure. According to Mrs. Beattie, this *is* the state in which the 'astral body' may pass out of the physical body. Is this, perhaps, the meaning of that curious passage at the beginning of Blake's *Europe*:

> Five windows light the cavern'd Man; thro' one he breathes the air;
> Thro' one hears music of the spheres; thro' one the eternal vine

Flourishes, that he may receive the grapes; thro' one
can look
And see small portions of the eternal world that ever
groweth;
Thro' one himself pass out what time he please; but
he will not,
For stolen joys are sweet, and bread eaten in secret
pleasant.

The opening lines are clear enough—they obviously
refer to the five senses. But what is this 'window through
which man can pass out what time he please'? And what
is the meaning of the odd line about stolen joys and
bread 'eaten in secret'? Is this not Powys's 'cavoseniargising' or 'mythologising,' withdrawing deep into some
secret place? Is Blake saying that *this* is the route to
passing out of the body?

The interesting thing about John Lilly's book is that
he quite obviously believes that his strange experiences
under LSD were more than 'imagination.' And he continues to emphasise the distinction between being 'in'
his body and out of it.

'Then I became intensely exhilarated and went into a
high while in my body. I got out of the tank and went
out into the sunlight, looking up into the sky, savoring
the fact that I was a human being on a planet. For the
first time since childhood, life was precious. My body
was precious. My feelings of energy and extreme ex-
hilaration continued. I sat and contemplated the wonder of our creation, of the creation of our planet. An
hour or so later, I climbed back into the tank and
launched into other regions. I had had enough of the
vast spaces, the vast entities for a while. Now I attempted to contact other systems of life, more on a level
with our own, and yet alien to us. I moved into a region
of strange life forms, neither above nor below the

human level, but strange beings, of strange shapes, metabolism, thought forms and so forth. . . . The vast variety of possible forms in the universe passed before me.'

Earlier in the book, John Lilly describes a crucial experience in which he came close to losing his life. In giving himself an antibiotic injection, he also injected a small quantity of detergent into his blood—the syringe had not been thoroughly cleaned out; the bubbles lodged in his brain, and he went into a coma. Fortunately, he was taken to a hospital where he was known, and eventually recovered. While in a coma, waiting for the ambulance, he had a sensation of coming into contact with two 'guardians':

'The pounding headache, the nausea and the vomiting that occurred forced me to leave my body. I became a focussed centre of consciousness and travelled into other spaces and met other beings, entities, or consciousnesses. I came across two who approached me through a large empty space, and who looked, felt and transmitted guiding and teaching thoughts to me.' He says of them: 'I realise that they are beings far greater than I. They begin to teach me. They tell me I can stay in this place, that I have left my body, that I can return to it if I wish. They then show me what would happen if I left my body back there—an alternative path for me to take. . . . They tell me it is not yet time for me to leave my body permanently, and that I still have an option to go back to it. They give me total and absolute confidence, total certitude in the truth of my being in this state. I know with certainty that they exist. . . .' And he adds: 'They say that they are my guardians, that they have been with me before at critical times, and that in fact they are with me always, but that I am not usually in a state to perceive them.'

Again, much of this sounded familiar to me. For example, a man named Ed Morrell, who was confined in a strait-jacket in a prison in Arizona. In fact, the treatment —designed to break the spirit of 'tough' prisoners—was to lace them tightly in two strait-jackets, one outside the other, and then pour water on them so they would shrink. It was like being 'slowly squeezed to death by a boa constrictor.' But at the height of the pain, he suddenly found himself wandering around outside the prison. Summarising this case in *The Phenomena of Astral Projection,* Muldoon and Carrington declare that while 'projecting,' Morrell met the Governor of the State, George W. P. Hunt, who was later able to verify what Morrell had seen at the time. Jack London made Morrell the hero of his book *The Star Rover.*

Similarly, the medium Ena Twigg (whose contacts with the dead son of Bishop James Pike are summarised in *The Occult*) has described in her autobiography (*Medium*) how, as a child of two or three, she could fly up and down the stairs after her body had been put to bed. She was always aware of entities who were apparently invisible to other people; she named these 'misty people.' At the age of fourteen, the 'misty people' told her that her father would be 'with them' in a week's time. Exactly a week later he slipped and fractured his skull, dying a few hours later. But until she was an adult, she remained only vaguely 'psychic.' The turning point came with a serious illness—appendicitis. Under anaesthetic, she was aware of herself suspended above her body, looking down. The operation was not wholly successful; she failed to gain weight after it, and gradually became weaker. One day, three of her 'misty people' walked into the bedroom. They seemed to be doctors; one wrote down what she told him about her symptoms; another gave her an injection in the base of the neck. The mark was there the next morning when she told her husband about the experience. The three 'guardians' came weekly, and her health recovered. She asked them how she could repay them. 'By helping others.' They gave her the address of a spiritualist circle.

Cases like this obviously do nothing to disprove or confirm the individual case of Mrs. Beattie. A sceptic would say they were all liars or victims of their imagination. On the other hand, if you accept that the sheer weight of the evidence tends to confirm that 'there are more things in heaven and earth' than Bertrand Russell ever suspected, then all these cases will be seen as part of a discernible pattern, and Mrs. Beattie's claims fit into this pattern.

On the second occasion Mrs. Beattie came to stay with us, I asked her how she'd slept. She said she hadn't slept much, because she'd had to spend the night helping someone in Sheffield. I pressed for further details. She said she had been 'summoned' to Sheffield to help someone she had never met; the woman was thinking of killing herself. Mrs. Beattie's task was to soothe her by standing beside her and pouring reassuring thoughts into her head. The guiding of the astral body, she said, was achieved by a kind of imaginative willing —a statement that agrees with most writers who have described astral projection.

Mrs. Beattie's observations struck me as rather more interesting than most of the accounts contained in Muldoon and Carrington—which are simply straightforward descriptions of out-of-the-body experiences. She is very much preoccupied with the evolutionary aspect of the whole experience. I had hoped to find a consecutive account of her 'cosmology' in the manuscripts; but they

moved from subject to subject. But here is a brief outline sketch, compiled from the manuscripts, and from
her answers on tape:

Human beings have three bodies: the physical body,
the energy body and the astral (or soul-) body. All our
memories are associated with the energy body. After
death, the astral body is freed; the energy body remains
in a state of quiescence or unconsciousness for three
days. The energy body is joined to the physical body at
the navel, and has its root in the liver. This body is
also called the Ka, the Egyptian word for it. The Ka
remains with the physical body to keep it alive when the
astral body travels. After death, the Ka gradually dis-
integrates as the physical body decomposes; its memories are transferred to the astral body at death. In
cases of violent death, the astral body finds itself in a
grey, misty place and feels confused and lost. Mrs.
Beattie has also helped to 'guide' these lost souls out of
this limbo state. 'Ghosts' are not lost souls, but fragments of the energy body which have not disintegrated.
This happens in cases of violent death, when the memory has not had time to be transferred to the soul-body.

The astral body has awareness of the 'subconscious'
mind. As human beings achieve extension of consciousness, they also achieve a closer relation to the subconscious mind. At a higher level still, the astral body
is in contact with the whole race memory, which can
become available to it. Interestingly enough, Mrs.
Beattie says that she disbelieves in reincarnation. People who think they have glimpsed themselves in previous
existences are actually contacting fragments of the race
memory. This is a point on which she is in flat disagreement with Arthur Guirdham, the subject of my next
chapter. But it is only fair to say that spiritualists in

general disagree about this subject. I asked Professor Wilson Knight if, next time he attended a seance, he would ask about reincarnation. He obliged me, and told me later that there seemed to be no general agreement. Reincarnation probably *did* occur, but it was the exception rather than the rule.

When Mrs. Beattie was in our house, she picked up a book called *A World Beyond* by Ruth Montgomery, purporting to be a description of the after-life, transmitted to Ruth Montgomery from the medium Arthur Ford, after his death. Mrs. Beattie opened it at a page dealing with race memory, and showed it to me, saying, 'Look, that's exactly what I was saying earlier.' It was; but on other points, there is considerable disagreement between Mrs. Beattie's 'world beyond' and Ruth Montgomery's. Ruth Montgomery states that reincarnation is definitely the rule, and that it is the means by which men work out 'evil karma' (although she doesn't use this phrase). For example, a philanthropist who had an appalling disfigurement on one side of his face had killed a child in a previous existence by striking it with great violence in the same place. . . .

After death, the soul feels as if it is travelling down a long tunnel, and then emerges into a region that is very much like this physical world. In a sense, they are still exactly the same person they were when alive; 'they don't become spiritual just because they've died.' Evil souls may fall into a kind of limbo, an outer darkness. (Ruth Montgomery explains that Hitler has fallen into this state, but that he propelled himself into it. The paranoid self-assertion continued in the 'world beyond,' but produced no effect, except increasing frustration and fury in Hitler—producing a fragmented mental state like insanity. . . .)

From the 'ordinary' (or 'earthly') level, souls may evolve to a level in which they become involved in useful work (the 'guardians'?). Beyond this, there are two higher levels. All children—souls of those who have died young—congregate at the third level. The fourth level is 'purely creative.' I found this slightly baffling—after all, creativity can exist on any level—but Mrs. Beattie explained that these four levels also exist in the minds of living people, i.e. we can evolve through these levels while still alive, and the level we have reached determines our place in the 'world beyond.'

At this point, Mrs. Beattie made some comments that I did not fully understand. 'We've got to grow, to balance the negative, unconscious forces. We've got to have three extensions of consciousness in our conscious minds to balance the three levels of unconscious forces.' She conceives the subconscious as negative. (Elsewhere in the manuscripts, there is an interesting table labelled 'Human polarisation,' which declares that in man, the physical body is positive, and in woman, negative. The energy body in man is negative, and in woman, positive. The soul- or astral body in man is positive, in woman, negative; and male consciousness is negative, while in woman, consciousness is positive. This, she says, is why man and woman harmonise, complementing each other.) When I asked her to explain the three negative forces of the unconscious more fully, she referred me to the manuscripts; but I have not been able to find anything.

But it seems to me that the essence of Mrs. Beattie's ideas is contained in a phrase she used when I asked her why some 'spiritual' people are completely non-psychic. 'We make an inward journey, to find the truth of our own being. You go through the emotional soul level, and in so doing, you become aware of the psychic level.'

A lot of what she says puzzles me, or simply rings no bells at all. But this phrase seemed to me to be of central importance: the inward journey. She says several times in the manuscript that most people live on a purely physical level, unaware that this is only an imitation of real life. In her teens—perhaps earlier—she learned the trick of 'cavoseniargising,' making the inward journey, focusing the inner-mind.

Anybody can do this. Ed Morrell did it by focusing on pain. I have heard of cases in which a similar act of focusing could bring a certain release. In America, I met a young college teacher who said he could induce sudden intense experiences of joy, and that he had learned this trick as a boy, when he had to sit still in church. One day, when he had been fidgeting, his mother told him he would be punished if he didn't stop it. Then he began to itch—I think he said it was in the small of his back—and experienced an overwhelming desire to scratch it, which he had to resist. The itch became unbearable—then, as he concentrated on it, was suddenly replaced by an intense 'peak experience.'

It is not necessary to focus on pain. If I settle down to read a book that I have been trying to obtain for a long time, or to listen to some music that I really want to hear, I relax completely, and prepare to devote my fullest attention to the act of focusing; and it is this that leads to states of absorption that resemble the mystic's contemplation. Such an act of concentration on one thing also refreshes us; no matter how weary I feel, if I become deeply interested in something, my energies slowly return. I recall, at the age of fifteen or so, cycling nearly fifty miles to Matlock Bath, in Derbyshire, and arriving there worn out. I felt that all I wanted to do was to lie down and sleep; instead, we paid our shillings and went on a guided tour of one of the deep caves that run below the limestone hills. It involved a great deal of walking and scrambling; yet we came out as relaxed and refreshed as if we'd had a good night's sleep. The proper use of our energies depends on this power to direct them—or rather, direct the attention—to new regions of the mind. This is the way 'mental voyages' are made; this is the way in which we explore our hidden powers. This is the reason people seek pleasure—because pleasure has the power to direct the mind in a single direction. And such a 'focusing' is, literally, a voyage. After a short time, we find ourselves in new mental realms, just as if we were exploring a road, and when we look back, we have an odd sense of being far from home—or at least, from the starting point.

For me, what is important about Mrs. Beattie is not her claim to be able to project the astral body, or her descriptions of the after-life. I am unable to judge these, not having any basis of personal experience to go on. But it seems clear to me that the rather odd, introspective girl who was brought up on a Welsh farm, developed the same power that all artists and poets possess: the power to make 'inward journeys' . . . and perhaps developed it to a greater extent than most. An artist might regard her as an artist *manqué,* but it seems to me that she would have as much right to regard the artist as a 'psychic *manqué.*' Both belong to the group of 'inward voyagers.' Mrs. Beattie is not a philosopher; but the central idea that emerges from her work is the basis of modern existentialist philosophy: Kierkegaard's recognition that 'truth is subjectivity.' But, expressed in this way, we fail to grasp its significance. What we are talking about is a *real* power that is possessed by human beings: the power to evolve by a process of 'inner voyage.'

She herself has a rather sceptical attitude towards a great deal of what she has written, and is obviously not sure how much of it comes from her own mind, and how much from 'outside.' She writes in her notes: 'The things I have written from time to time, when the mood was on me, seem to me not typical of me. Some is too donnish, other pieces are too sentimental. (It all has a religious background, which *is*, of course, me.) But I rather suspect the other material, which is why I don't know what to do with it. It's all broken up. . . .'

This may be true, but it does not matter. What is significant about her is that she has learned the trick of making 'inner voyages' without the aid of a water-tank or psychedelic drugs, and she demonstrates that it *can* be done. I think that she is right to believe that she has taken a step along the road that leads to the next phase of human evolution.

CHAPTER THREE

DR. ARTHUR GUIRDHAM

I had just completed *The Occult*—some time around August 1970—when I saw a review of a book called *The Cathars and Reincarnation* by Arthur Guirdham. It was a short review, but it said that it was probably the best authenticated case of reincarnation on record. So I hastened to buy the book, which was published by Spearman—a firm that seemed to have succeeded Rider as England's chief 'occult' publishers.

The book arrived in mid-September. It had a sub-title: 'The record of a past life in 13th century France.' I settled down to read it; from the blurb, it sounded fascinating.

My first impression was one of disappointment. The writer began by stating that one of his patients—he was a doctor—had written down all kinds of details about the Cathars, a heretical sect of the twelfth and thirteenth centuries, and that at the time she wrote, most of these details were unknown to scholars. Since that time—twenty-six years ago—many of these details have been verified, said Dr. Guirdham. . . . He certainly had my attention. In fact, it seemed fairly clear to me that he had the material of a best-seller. All he had to do was to tell his story simply, in chronological sequence.

Unfortunately, this was precisely what he didn't do. His style was clear enough, but he got involved in all kinds of minor details about the Cathars and thirteenth-century France until I was completely bogged down. What it needed was to tell the reader, in words of one syllable, exactly who the Cathars were, and their history up to the time of their destruction by the Inquisition. And then, step by step, to tell the story of his patient, whom he calls Mrs. Smith, and show how it corresponded in detail with what is known of the Cathars in Languedoc in the middle of the thirteenth century— particularly of the murder of the two Inquisitors at Avignonet in 1242, which led to the great persecution of Cathars, culminating in the massacre of Montségur.

On the other hand, the very fact that he hadn't tried to turn the book into another *Search for Bridey Murphy* was evidence for the genuineness of the book. I got the impression that, as a doctor, he was slightly embarrassed by the sensational nature of the material he was presenting, and was anxious to present it as soberly as possible.

The story presented in *The Cathars and Reincarnation* is, briefly, as follows:

Throughout his adult life, Arthur Guirdham has felt a strong attraction to the heretical sect known as the Cathars, or 'pure ones.' Their basic doctrine was similar to that of the Manichees and the Gnostics: that this world is the domain of Satan, and that human beings are the spirits of angels who revolted against God, and who have been condemned to spend a lifetime imprisoned in the body. This world is hell, created by the devil. A man's only chance of redemption is to become united with Christ in this life, to become completely pure.

The Catholic church has always been inclined to condemn this type of doctrine; to begin with, the Bible says that God looked at the world and saw that it was good. Second, the majority of clerics, from priests to popes, have been ordinary human beings, lacking in fanaticism; the Savonarolas and Cornelius Jansens strike them as slightly nutty. On the other hand, intense natures long to evolve at a faster rate than the church makes provision for, and this has been the source of all the Church's troubles, from Chrysostom to Luther. The 'purists,' the fanatics, are a nuisance and a menace. Purist doctrines always made their strongest appeal in times of universal hardship and suffering; and at the time of the second Crusade, there was plenty of hardship and suffering in Europe.

Trouble began after 1174, when St. Bernard preached against the Cathars in Toulouse, which was virtually their capital city; Count Raymond of Toulouse was a Cathar. In 1205, a monk called Dominic Guzman—later Saint Dominic—began his own personal crusade against the Cathars, wandering around barefoot and preaching against them. His followers—the Dominicans—were later given the job of rooting out Catharism, and became known as the Inquisition. In 1204, the pope asked the king of France to depose Count Raymond and place a good Catholic in his position. In 1208, one of Raymond's squires retaliated by assassinating the papal legate; the pope was so furious that he couldn't speak for two days. And the first 'crusade' against the Cathars began in 1209. Twenty thousand people were massacred at Béziers. Simon de Montfort (senior—father of the founder of English democracy) was a particularly violent persecutor. He plundered Toulouse in 1215. The slaughter and persecution went on, with Toulouse changing hands, for the next thirty years. But the beginning of the end happened in 1242, when the two

Inquisitors were betrayed by their host, and murdered. In 1243, the Cathars were besieged at Montségur; they held out for ten months; when they finally surrendered, two hundred who refused to renounce their faith were burned alive in one huge pyre.

All this is necessary to understand Arthur Guirdham's book—and Arthur Guirdham. For he reached the conclusion that his obsessive interest in Catharism, and in the Montségur area, was due to the fact that he had been a Cathar 'priest' named Roger de Grisolles during this final period of persecution.

He reached this conclusion in a rather odd way. Throughout his life, he had had nightmares in which he was asleep in a room when a tall man approached him; sometimes he would wake up screaming. In March 1962, he saw a priest who had been suffering from a very similar nightmare: Mrs. 'Smith.' Her shrieks were so loud that her husband was afraid she would wake up the street. The doctor who had referred her to Arthur Guirdham had at one time wondered if she was epileptic. In fact, Mrs. Smith's nightmares ceased when she met Guirdham. (His nightmares ceased at roughly the same time.) She didn't tell him this, for she wanted to continue as his patient—for a rather odd reason. She had recognised him as a man she knew well from her dreams.

Mrs. Smith hesitated for some time before she finally told Guirdham her full story. What emerged, finally, was this. As a child she had possessed a remarkable memory; during an exam she was able to write out page after page of Wordsworth, so that she was accused of cheating. At the age of eleven she became unconscious with a severe headache; when she woke up, she had a degree of second sight; she knew when her father would die; she knew that a friend's marriage would not take place; she knew what was in letters before opening them. During her teens, she had three more attacks of unconsciousness—which were diagnosed as epileptic fits; then she began to have the curious, detailed dreams of her previous life in the thirteenth century. She was a girl of humble background who lived with her family in a single-room house near Toulouse.

One night, a man had arrived at the house, and asked for shelter. This was the Cathar 'priest,' Roger de Grisolles (or Roger Isarn). The young girl—Mrs. Smith—fell in love with him. (Oddly enough, the dreams did not include her real name—Guirdham calls her Puerilia.) She crept over to him in the night and kissed his hand. The two became friendly. One day, her father beat her, and she left home and went to Roger's house, where she became his mistress. (Roger was not a fully fledged priest, or a 'parfait'—Cathars who had forsworn sex.)

Then, in Mrs. Smith's dream, there was a murder. A man came back from the murder, boasting about it; his name was Pierre de Mazerolles. Later, Roger was arrested, and died in prison. Mrs. Smith—or rather Puerilia—was burned at the stake. She also dreamed of this burning—in gruesome detail, with her blood dripping into the flames, and her eyelids burned off.

All kinds of names occurred in Mrs. Smith's dreams. Now, there *are* still records extant of the period—of the trials of Cathars, and so on. So Arthur Guirdham's task was to study the records, and see if Mrs. Smith's dreams made sense. He quickly discovered that Pierre de Mazerolles *was* one of the men involved in the murder of the two Inquisitors. He was able to identify Roger, and his parents and other members of the family. Mrs. Smith's story definitely held together. Not only that, but her notes, written so many years earlier, contained material about the Cathars that was not known to scholars at the time, and has only since then been confirmed.

Altogether, I found *The Cathars and Reincarnation* a puzzling, difficult book. Not long after buying it, I realised that I had a couple more books by Arthur Guirdham on my shelves: *A Theory of Disease* and *The Nature of Healing*. I had bought them at the time I had been writing my study of Rasputin and the fall of the Romanovs—I had asked Professor Wilson Knight's advice on books about thaumaturgic healing, and he had recommended these and a couple by Harry Edwards. At the time, they had failed to strike a chord, and I had forgotten I had them. Now I opened *A Theory of Disease* (1957) again, I recalled what had dissatisfied me at the time I read it. It holds the rather unusual thesis that disease is often due to the degree to which a person is preoccupied with his own personality. Shaw's Saint Joan remarks, 'Thinking about yourself is like thinking about your stomach—it's the quickest way to make yourself sick.' So I could understand his basic thesis— the relation of disease to self-awareness. At the same time, according to this thesis, 'outsiders' ought to be far more subject to disease than most people. And while it is true that a large number of artists and poets of the nineteenth century died of tuberculosis, I couldn't see otherwise that outsiders are more disease-prone than the average; on the contrary, they're often less so. I thought of the occasion when Strindberg determined to commit suicide by getting pneumonia, so he flung himself into icy water, then climbed a tall tree, and crouched in the cold wind all night. In the morning he staggered off and found a bed, expecting to wake up dying; instead he woke up feeling in the best of health.

But now I re-read the book, I realised that this argument doesn't affect its thesis. The whole point about 'outsiders' is that, in spite of feeling isolated from society, and perhaps from life itself, they often possess remarkable depths of toughness. Having got over that misunderstanding, I found *A Theory of Disease* a remarkable book. (I still think it is in many ways his best.) When it came out in 1957, it must have been regarded as extremely unorthodox, even though many psychologists recognised the mental origin of many physical diseases. But there was a tendency to blame disease on sexual repressions. Now, Guirdham makes the controversial statement that apart from the 'personality,' with its self-obsession, there is a layer of our being that could be called 'the You that is Not You.' (I had once expressed this by saying that man possesses a personality, which is oriented towards self-satisfaction, and an Impersonality, which can get a pure and impersonal delight out of mathematics or a sunset.) Health may depend on contact with this layer. The mentally ill patient often says: 'I cannot get away from myself. I think only of myself.' 'It would be better . . . if the doctor were able to instruct the patient in some meditative and spiritual technique whereby he could limit the operations of his personality by merging himself with the absolute. . . . Modern medicine had its beginnings in the Greek temples. It may have to return to the temple for its salvation. . . .' But what makes the book so fascinating is the author's analysis of various types of diseases, and of the way these relate to various levels of the personality. Most books that relate healing to the 'spiritual' are rather airy-fairy and unrealistic; Guirdham's book has a strong flavour of reality.

The Nature of Healing, published seven years after *A Theory of Disease,* goes a great deal further—which is obviously why Wilson Knight had recommended it to me. He is concerned with the gift of healing, such as was possessed by Rasputin; you might say that he is in the field of Christian Science. He has obviously reached a watershed, and I could easily trace the route by which he arrived at it. Everybody must have noticed the way that certain people are totally preoccupied with themselves, in a feverish, unhealthy way, and that such people seem unable to draw upon their full powers; they seem to be cut off from their inner resources; whereas people who exude calm and serenity—and health—are often curiously un-egoistic. In fact, they often possess the power to heal. (Think of Matthew Arnold's line about Wordsworth's healing power—connected with his awareness of 'unknown modes of being,' of things *outside* himself.) In *A Theory of Disease,* Guirdham is preoccupied with working out the implications of these observations. In *The Nature of Healing,* he goes on to consider the way that Negro 'medicine men' can cause death by laying a curse on someone, and how aborigines may wilt away and die because someone has 'pointed the bone' at them. Any psychologist would accept this, and would say that it is purely psychological. But if this is so, then how far is all disease purely psychological? And if we accept that purely psychological forces are involved in disease, can we discount the possibility of such forces being 'projected' by a medicine man in order to cause disease? Is it not possible that such forces are as real, if as invisible, as germs?

In *The Nature of Healing,* Guirdham also touches on reincarnation; describing a nurse with unusual healing powers, he comments that she knew the layout of Hampton Court long before she went there, so that visiting it was like going home; she was convinced that she had had some intense experience of happiness in the garden at Hampton Court in 1660. 'She knew the London of

Charles the Second better than that of today,' and as a child, she made drawings of Norman architecture, with the same odd sense of familiarity. Guirdham adds: 'I am convinced that the power of healing which she undoubtedly possessed involves the capacity to disperse oneself through time.'

These two books made it clear to me that Guirdham was not a crank—or perhaps just given to wishful thinking. There is a feeling of clarity, balance, fair-mindedness, about them. He had obviously come a long way, and come very slowly; he mentions that in the past he had been completely sceptical about the possibility of 'healing' except by purely physical (or natural) forces.

At about the time I was reading these books, an old friend, Tom Greenwell, came to stay with us; he works on the *Yorkshire Post,* and he brought with him a pamphlet called *Catharism: The Mediaeval Resurgence of Primitive Christianity,* by Arthur Guirdham. This, I felt, was beginning to look more like synchronicity than coincidence. *The Cathars and Reincarnation* begins by describing how Guirdham kept stumbling upon references to Catharism all over the place. One day, he was discussing a village, and tried to recall the name of its pub; later the same day, he took a book on the Pyrenees out of the public library—and came across the name of the village and its pub in it. I felt that the pamphlet on the Cathars—and the fact that Tom Greenwell had met Guirdham at the time when he was contributing medical articles to the *Yorkshire Post*—clearly indicated that I ought to write to him. I did so, saying how much I had enjoyed the book, but that I felt he had deliberately thrown away the possibility of a best-seller. A few days later, I got a friendly letter back, in which he said that he had deliberately played down the sensational elements—which is what I had suspected.

I wrote a section about him in *The Occult,* as well as an article for the back page of *Man, Myth and Magic.* By that time, we had finally met. In the spring of 1971, he drove down to the west country to visit relatives, and came to stay overnight. The final paragraph of my article on him read: 'Earlier this year, he came down to stay with us. My mental picture of him had varied between the image of a keen-eyed psychiatrist, and of an absent-minded mystic. He was neither of these things: a gentle, intelligent man with the natural kindness that all good doctors have. Throughout the first evening, while we talked mostly about psychology, I felt that there was an element about him that I could not place. Later on, it came to me: there was something priestly about him, something akin to Father Brown, or one of those mediaeval priors described by Rabelais.'

This, I think, is a fairly good description. He is white-haired, rather squarely built—he points out in the healing book that many healers are—with a calm, rather soothing voice. He reminded me of another old medical friend, Kenneth Walker, who had been a pupil of Guirdjieff's. He had his wife Mary with him, and she struck me as an ideal sort of person for a doctor's wife: calm, good-tempered, practical and thoroughly efficient. She and Joy seemed to have a certain amount in common; writers, like doctors, tend to become objects of fixation for people who imagine they hold the solution to all their problems. Their wives have to learn to put up with this, and to adopt a philosophical attitude, particularly to female admirers; you can read in their eyes a kind of mild, patient irony. In a way, Mary Guirdham convinced me more than her husband that Arthur Guirdham wasn't over-credulous or over-inventive. She struck me as so balanced and intelligent that I couldn't believe she would aid and abet any kind of self-deception.

We talked, as I have said, mainly about psychology. I was writing *New Pathways in Psychology,* and I was struck by the similarity of Maslow's views and Arthur Guirdham's. Translated into Maslow's language, you could say that Arthur Guirdham believed that disease was due to blockage of creative energies—that is, blockage of self-actualisation. But then, in a way, Guirdham went further than Maslow. When Maslow died, he was looking into this question of the varieties of self-actualisation—what Robert Leftwich might call the structure of the superconscious. Maslow was concerned only with learning to express creative energy: i.e. to evolve. Arthur Guirdham seemed to be implying that evolution of consciousness may involve us in the realm of 'strange powers.' All the same, it was not the 'strange powers' we talked about that evening, but the psychotherapy of men like Maslow and Viktor Frankl. I was particularly fascinated by a story told by Robert Ardrey about two scientists, Rubinstein and Best, who had discovered that planarion worms are subject to boredom and 'life failure' if made to repeat a task over and over again. But by making the task so difficult that the worms have to make an enormous effort to learn it, they were able to make the worms repeat it hundreds of times without boredom. Somehow, the worms came to attach *meaning* to the task when they had to really summon their vitality to learn it, and this meaning stayed permanently, uneroded by repetition. Clearly, the question of disease and health is closely connected with the question of meaning and boredom. Disease is basically the outcome of life-failure.

Arthur disclaimed any healing powers of his own, and any 'psychic' ability. He was, he said, just a catalyst, the sort of person who seems to bring out 'strange powers' in other people. But he certainly possesses a degree of natural, if not supernatural, healing power. I had de-

veloped a rather odd pain at the back of my skull. There
was a slight ache in the muscles of the right rear-side of
my neck and a sharp pain at the back of the head in
moments of excitement, such as sexual orgasm. Arthur
stood behind my chair, and gently massaged the muscles
of the neck and shoulders for a few minutes; after this,
the stiffness vanished, and stayed away for about a week.
There was a definitely soothing feeling as he pressed the
muscles.

My ten-year-old daughter took an immediate and
warm liking to him—so much so that she asked him if
he would mind being her godfather. She'd been looking
out for a godfather for some time, ever since we'd called
on the godfather of her brother Damon—the Blake
scholar Foster Damon—at Annisquam, Mass. Arthur
seemed agreeable; he is now Sally's godfather. . . .

The only other thing I recollect about his two-day
visit is that he talked a great deal about the South of
France, and places he'd visited; he also produced some
bottles of an odd sweet champagne from the Languedoc.
I don't particularly like travel, and traveller's tales usually bore me; but there was something about his description of small French villages in the Midi—the heat and
the laziness and the local wines—that fascinated me. It
was obvious that he loved the area—that, in a way, he
was obsessed by it.

Later in the year, I visited the Guirdhams at their
home near Bath—we were driving back from the north
of England. We were only staying overnight, so there
wasn't time for a great deal of talk; but he told me that
he was working on an even more remarkable story than
that of 'Mrs. Smith'—a record of a whole group of incarnations. He let me see some of the manuscript. As I
read the first page, I began to feel—no, not excited; that
would be the wrong word; a kind of satisfaction, as when

something turns out very much to your liking. This manuscript—which I have with me now as I write—was clearer and more straightforward than the earlier book on reincarnation. And it raised and answered most of the questions—and doubts—that had occurred to me as I read the earlier book. He says on the first page:

'I am naturally of a sceptical and cautious nature, and am known in my family as Doubting Thomas. I am astonished that the phenomena I have encountered have been revealed to me of all people. I have occupied myself in discovering the significance of names and messages produced in dreams, visions, in states of clairaudience and dictated by discarnate entities. Because of the unusual origin of my data I have to stress all the more carefully that I was for forty years a run-of-the-mill psychiatrist. In the National Health Service I was the Senior Consultant in my clinical area. I hold a scientific degree, as well as being a doctor of medicine. It is all the more necessary to make these points since I claim that this, my own story, is, of its kind, the most remarkable I have encountered.'

And in the first chapter, he makes an observation that aroused my interest: that most of the cases of reincarnation he has come across were rather healthy, active people with 'more than average energy'; not, as you might expect, 'sick sensitives.' This is certainly what I would have predicted, on the basis of the psychology I have developed in *New Pathways*. Knowledge of previous existences is certainly not necessary to our everyday survival; all we need is a narrow, commonplace consciousness. Flashes of this kind of knowledge would only come, like 'peak experiences,' to very healthy people, with energy to spare.

I was also intrigued by something he says about Miss Mills, an acquaintance who asked him one day whether

the words 'Raymond' and 'Albigensian' meant anything
to him. (They kept recurring in her head.) Miss Mills
mentioned childhood dreams—following an illness—of
running away from a castle, and of being led towards
a stake with heaped faggots. She commented that, as a
child, the rest of the family had enjoyed the spectacle
of a building on fire, while she had been hysterical. I
recall similar feelings in my own childhood. There was
a weekly serial on at the local cinema, with a character
called the Eagle—a Lone Ranger type who always found
himself in some dangerous situation at the end of every
episode. But one day, he was trapped in a burning
church; and I was so horrified that I couldn't bear to
ever watch him again. Not long after *The Occult* came
out, a friend asked me if he could bring someone along
to meet me, a woman who ran a nursing home in Cornwall, and who was interested in occult matters. We spent
an interesting evening talking about all kinds of things;
but at one point, she suddenly told me that she was certain I had been a monk in a previous existence, and had
been burned to death. . . .

In many respects, Arthur Guirdham's account of his
experiences with Miss Mills parallels that of his experiences with 'Mrs. Smith.' Miss Mills would wake up in
the night with names in her head—names like Montserver, Braida, Cisilia; these he was able to identify,
through his knowledge of the siege of Montségur and
the burning of the heretics two days after its surrender.
After a while, she would find notes written on a notepad
she kept by her bed, scrawled in a hand resembling her
own. One said: 'Raymond de Perella. Sun—No. Treasure—No. Books—Yes.' Arthur Guirdham interpreted
this as a reference to questions about Montségur. It had
been suggested that Montségur had been the site of a
sun-worship temple; Miss Mills's 'instructor' was appar-

ently denying this. As to the treasure of Montségur, this is another question debated by historians. Four 'parfaits' (the highest Cathar grade) were lowered from the walls of the citadel just before its surrender, carrying unspecified 'treasure.' It has been suggested that this was money, or even the Holy Grail. Miss Mills's instructor was asserting that the 'treasure' consisted of Cathar sacred books.

In his eighth chapter, Guirdham has an interesting and important discussion of a basic doctrinal point: reincarnation. He comments that many of the biblical quotations dictated to Miss Mills were from St. Paul—which, he says, is natural enough, since St. Paul is the 'supreme interpreter of Christianity from the occult point of view'—an observation that had certainly never occurred to me. Paul lays emphasis on the difference between the corporeal body and the spiritual body. Guirdham says: 'His outlook tied up directly with modern conceptions of etheric and astral bodies and the like. Orthodox Christians may jib at the idea that early Christianity was characterised by psychic communication and spiritist phenomena. What was to be revealed later to Miss Mills indicated clearly that primitive Christianity was of this nature.' He goes on to state that the verse from Corinthians I (Chapter 15, verse 45) '. . . the first Adam was made a living soul, the last Adam was made a quickening spirit' is specifically Cathar, although orthodox Christians tend to accept it without really asking what it means. 'This particular verse implies that a living soul is in man from the beginning. . . . Man is born with his full psychic complement. This is an essential feature of the doctrine of reincarnation. After death, the psyche does not pass into any such state of cosmic somnolence as is represented by limbo. It embarks on a process of reincarnation. 'The last Adam was made a quickening spirit' refers to our ultimate development in being emancipated from matter. To the Cathars, this was the raison d'être of our existence. They recognised that there was every gradation between matter conceived of as inert spirit, and, at the other extreme, as so spiritualised that Christ could appear on earth and reveal the true nature of his spiritualised body to the disciples at the Transfiguration.'

But I must move on to the central point of this strange book. The adjective 'strange' is an understatement. It is either a piece of sheer nuttiness, or one of the most important books ever written. For its central assertion is that a whole *group* of Cathars from Montségur have been reincarnated in England in the twentieth century. Miss Mills was only the first. And although she began by having to ask Guirdham whether Raymond and Albigensian meant anything to him, she ended by actually *seeing* Braida de Montserver, a 'parfaite' (i.e. a kind of female priest) who was burned; Braida began to pay her nightly visits, and instruct her in the history, philosophy and healing techniques of Catharism. Later, she was visited by two male Cathars, Guilhabert de Castres, and a bishop, Bertrand de Marty. And here, we might say, the plot thickens. Miss Mills became convinced that Bertrand Marty was her father—that is to say, that her own twentieth-century father had been a reincarnation of Marty.

In October 1971, Miss Mills was contacted by a friend from the Midlands, whom Guirdham calls simply 'Betty.' Betty's husband had died of a heart attack, and she was badly shaken. She decided to take a holiday abroad—in the Pyrenees. Guirdham was asked to supply names of places worth visiting. Inevitably, many were associated with Catharism. Betty went to the Pyrenees, and apparently found the experience profoundly satisfy-

ing. And on her return to England, she began to mention
names of thirteenth-century Cathars that soon convinced
Miss Mills that here was yet another character from
Montségur, reincarnated in twentieth-century England.
Unfortunately, before this exciting new development
could be studied, Betty died of a stroke. Her mother,
Jane, began sorting through her papers, and found references to various names—Braida, Isarn, and so on. She
also discovered drawings made by Betty as a child—during a serious illness at the age of seven. These drawings,
mostly of a crude, matchstick variety, contain references
to people present at the siege of Montségur, and are full
of Cathar references. They seemed to trigger off some reaction—or buried memory—in Jane, who now herself
began 'recalling' her own life in the thirteenth century in
snatches.

Another person enters the story—an old schoolfriend
of Miss Mills's named Kathleen. She enquired after Betty
—whom she had also known—and on being told she
was dead, described a dream in which she had seen
Betty in a wood with a man dressed in dark blue with a
chain around his waist. . . . This man was actually
Guirdham's earlier incarnation, Roger Isarn; Guirdham
goes into the evidence for this with his usual scholarly
precision. It becomes clear that Kathleen is another of
the group of reincarnated Cathars.

And there are still more to come. There is Penelope,
who had been a business associate of Miss Mills's some
years ago. One evening, Penelope died unexpectedly, a
hundred miles from Bath; Miss Mills, who was with
Guirdham at the time, had a sudden powerful premoni-
tion that 'something is happening to somebody.' Penelope's husband Jack said that the last word she spoke
was 'Brasillac'—the name of a sergeant-at-arms who
fought at Montségur, and had been burned at the stake.

Jack came to call on Miss Mills, describing his wife's dreams of a castle on a hill, of men dressed in blue robes; he also spoke of her horror of fire, and of having stones thrown at her. (The castle was bombarded with stones thrown by giant catapults.) After this, Jack himself began to have dreams of fighting in a castle on the hill, accompanied by names. Guirdham finally concluded that Jack was Brasillac, and that his wife Penelope had been his sweetheart in his thirteenth-century existence. . . .

At the end of the book, Guirdham mentions that Miss Mills continues to practise 'healing,' under Braida's direction, and he concludes:

'To me, as a doctor, there is something of specific importance transmitted by Braida's messages. Dualism is an important antidote to the materialism of medicine. The next step in our evolution as doctors is to recognise more the influence of the psyche imprisoned in matter. Its recollections of experiences in past lives are related to present symptoms. The recognition of two basic energies of good and evil is vital to any cosmic concept of medicine. Healing is a particular expression of the emanation of goodness. On the other hand, it is indisputable that many disease symptoms and syndromes are attributable to the power of evil. Discussing such factors is beyond the scope of this book. All one can say here is that Braida's messages enlarged enormously one's medical horizons.'

Obviously, this book—entitled *We Are One Another* —answers the basic objections that can be made to *Cathars and Reincarnation*. It is possible to accept that a patient should have detailed memories of a previous existence in the thirteenth century; but much more difficult to believe that the doctor himself is a reincarnation of a man with whom the patient was involved seven hundred years ago. It also presents a problem for the total sceptic, who is inclined to dismiss the whole thing as self-delusion or downright lies. Arthur Guirdham is an intelligent man; this was plain to me from his books, before I met him; if he is inventing the whole thing, why should he go out of his way to make his story unbelievable? *We Are One Another* reveals that the Puerilia-Roger relation is just part of a much larger pattern; it would seem that dozens of the Cathars of Montségur have been reincarnated in the twentieth century for a specific purpose. The purpose, presumably, is to prove the reality of reincarnation.

Let us agree that both explanations—the sceptical and the nonsceptical—fit the facts as presented in these two books. A *News of the World* reporter—the kind who publishes investigations of mediums, healers and astrologers—would have no difficulty explaining what has happened. Guirdham has always been an unorthodox doctor, with tendencies to occultism. He becomes interested in the Cathars and Catharism. And when Mrs. Smith talks to him about her own thirteenth-century incarnations, he is willing to believe that he was her lover. In fact, of course, all that has happened is that a patient has become fixated on her doctor, and looks around for ways to gain his interest. . . . Miss Mills is also, significantly, an unmarried lady. She gets drawn into the fantasy, and she draws others into it, until a whole group of her friends are convinced that they were thirteenth-century Cathars. An interesting case of group hysteria or group suggestibility. . . .

Now, Guirdham is fully aware of these objections, and he takes a great deal of trouble in both books to emphasise that the complex facts cannot be accounted for by suggestibility or even by telepathy. Mrs. Smith's notes about the Cathars date back to her childhood, and various historical details—which she mentioned in the notes —were not even known to scholars at the time. A great deal of space in both these books is taken up with the examination of such details, which makes them, in some ways, rather tedious for the ordinary lay reader. If one accepts the genuineness of Betty's notes and drawings in the second book, then it is quite impossible that she could have been drawn into the fantasy by Miss Mills.

In fact, the only sceptical hypothesis that can be regarded as unassailable is that Guirdham himself has invented the whole thing: that neither Mrs. Smith, Miss Mills, Betty, Jane and the rest ever existed. And on my own knowledge of the Guirdhams, I find this almost impossible to accept. For what it is worth—and I agree it would not convince the *News of the World* reporter— he strikes me as eminently sane, balanced and honest.

Miss Mills told Guirdham that it was important to go ahead with the publication of the facts about this strange case, because the same kind of thing is happening all over the world at the moment, and it is important that other people involved should realise that they are not the only ones. In which case, it could be argued that it is in Guirdham's interest—and those of the 'Cathars'— to try to furnish some solid proofs. He mentions several times that Miss Mills had been unwilling to discuss her own experiences, even when some of the others involved —Betty, Jane, Jack—offered evidence that suggested that they themselves were Cathars. On the other hand, Miss Mills is obviously the key to the problem. At a fairly early stage in their acquaintance, she experienced a pain in her hip, and when Guirdham examined her, he found that she had a strange line of blisters across her back—hard blisters. This, said Miss Mills, was where she had been struck across the back with a burning torch as she was led to the stake. The blisters would certainly be very powerful corroborative evidence for the story.

However, let me, for the moment, put aside the doubts and qualifications, and ask the vital question: *If* this is all true, what does it mean?

Centrally, it would establish the fact of reincarnation, as certainly as Newton's observations established the fact of gravity. Which, even in occult circles, would cause a sensation. For, as I have already commented, by no means all spiritualists accept reincarnation—in fact, very few of them do. Mrs. Beattie seems inclined to deny it completely. On the other hand, there is a great deal of solid evidence for something of the sort. In *The Occult,* I quote *Twenty Cases Suggestive of Reincarnation* by Ian Stevenson M.D., published by the American Society for Psychical Research in 1966. This is one of those typically careful, painstaking volumes that offer huge quantities of detailed information about cases of supposed reincarnation. In a typical case, an Indian girl of seven described to her parents her previous existence in a nearby town, which she had never visited. She said that she had been a mother, and had died in childbirth. Taken to the town in question, she was able to point out people and places in a way that demonstrated that she certainly had a thorough knowledge of them, and was able to talk to relatives of her previous 'self' in the local dialect, although she had only been taught Hindustani. In the case of a Hindu boy who had been beheaded at the age of six by a relative who wanted to inherit property that would descend to the child, the 'reincarnated' boy had a scar on his neck resembling a knife wound. Another child who began to describe a previous existence (at the age of two) had scars on his stomach resembling gunshot wounds; he claimed to have been killed (in his previous existence) by a gun blast in the abdomen. All this would seem to support Guirdham's statements about his reincarnated Cathars suffering the pains of their burning and developing blisters.

Even if I did not know Arthur Guirdham, and consider him honest, I would still be inclined to give credit to his two Cathar books in the light of his other work. *A Theory of Disease* shows him, quite simply, breaking away from the Freudianism and behaviourism that form the foundation of every psychiatrist's medical training. Like Jung and Rank, he is groping towards 'holistic' concepts. And the holistic trend has been steadily gaining force in science and philosophy ever since Husserl formulated Phenomenology in 1912 and the gestalt psychologists began their experiments in perception. *Man, Divine or Social* (1960) is a determined attempt to formulate a kind of metaphysics of 'holism.' He again starts from the recognition of the 'You that is Not You' —what Husserl would call the transcendental ego. This book is about the conflict between man's two basic urges: what he calls 'the cosmic urge' and the Herd-Personality Impulse. This is less 'metaphysical' than it sounds. Wordsworth's poem 'The world is too much with us' deals with the same problem. (So does my *Outsider*.) Observed purely objectively—phenomenologically— man is a dual being, torn between 'the triviality of everydayness' (to use Heidegger's phrase) and sudden flashes of deeper meanings, 'a certain odour on the wind.' The problem is 'close-upness,' being forced to live with our noses pressed against reality. His use of the term 'Herd-Personality Impulse' indicates that he is preoccupied with the 'outsider' problem and how to solve it.

One of his most revealing books is a short work—a mere 95 pages—published in 1966 under the pseudonym Francis Eaglesfield; it is called *Silent Union, A Record of Unwilled Communication*, and consists of extracts from his journals about patients who had 'occult faculties.' For example, a rugger-playing coal merchant, who had often dreamed of things before they happened. When he followed the beagles, this man never had to look in the newspaper to see what time the hunt would start; he seemed to know intuitively, and would set out at the right time. This book forms a link between the early healing books and the later 'occult' books. Many of its cases are simply 'odd.' For example, the rather repressed, silent man who blamed himself for the death of his seven-year-old son—he had failed to call the doctor soon enough. His son had had a wart on his forehead, and the father often felt it with his index finger as he stroked the boy's forehead. One day, ten years after the boy's death, the father developed a wart on the fingertip; then they spread across the hand. A doctor burned off one wart with caustic; after this, the man called on an amateur wart charmer, who made the others 'disappear' very quickly. The incident demonstrates that warts may be cured, as well as caused by psychological strain.

But the most interesting and significant section of the book is its longest chapter, 25. He begins by describing an odd occurrence when he was on holiday in Yorkshire with Mary. They were staying at a hotel, and had been to visit a friend at a town fifteen miles away. They had only been driving home about four minutes when they passed a signpost saying that their destination was only three miles away. This seemed impossible; they stopped and looked in the A.A. book—which confirmed that the towns were fifteen miles apart. A few minutes later, they found themselves driving into the town—even the last three miles had 'vanished,' or been foreshortened. Time had somehow accelerated.

He goes on to describe the hotel they were staying in: 'there was something fascinating and macabre in its per-

fection of mediocrity.' Yet one evening, looking up from
his book in the lounge, everyone seemed to be intensely
alive, 'and endowed suddenly with a new and inexplic-
able dignity.' It was after these two events that he began
to keep a diary, the diary he quotes in this book.

The events seem, in a way, trivial. But they are of
considerable significance. The first indicates the illusory
and relative nature of time; the second, the relative
nature of our perception of the external world. Nothing
could seem 'realler' than the dullness of a lot of ordinary middle-class people, apparently incapable of an
original thought—or any thought at all. Something happens in the brain, a kind of psychic orgasm, and they
are transfigured. It is as if a new 'eye' had opened in
the brain.

He goes on to recount two more odd events. One we
already know about. In a couple of pages, without any
details about Cathars (or his own involvement) he
recounts the story of Mrs. Smith, calling her D; he mentions simply that her detailed account of a previous
existence convinced him of reincarnation. He also mentions an old friend, Celia, in whose presence he has always felt refreshed, 'as if I had been charged by an
inexhaustible battery.' But Celia had a deep distrust
of anything 'psychic,' and disliked Mrs. Smith's influence (such as it was). On a walk with Celia one day,
Guirdham felt completely low and exhausted, as if re-
covering from a serious illness, and felt like this for
several days. He concluded that Celia had, in some
way, withdrawn her psychic energy. Again, a minor
event—pointing only to the mind's power to give
strength and to heal.

There is another brief and interesting episode. His
wife asked him what he thought Keats looked like;
and then, a few minutes later, what was the next line

after 'Fear no more the heat of the sun' from *Cymbeline*. Ten minutes later, in a book on Napoleon, she came across a reference to Keats, and the song in *Cymbeline*.

And why should these disparate episodes be grouped together? Because, I think, they all point to the same thing: a 'bridge period' in life in which some fundamental change occurs. As far as I know, no one has ever written about the importance of 'bridge periods.' During these periods, you sense that something is happening, some basic change, of the sort that occurs at puberty. But then, when the body changes at puberty, you are aware that this is a purely subjective change; it is happening to you, not to the rest of the world. But in other 'bridge periods,' there is a curious feeling that can only be described as 'involvement,' as if you are involved in some wider, more general change. It is the kind of 'sense of change' you might experience if you drove down from New York to Florida in midwinter, and saw the scenery becoming greener, and felt the air becoming warmer. I am not implying that 'the world' is somehow taking account of you; only that you seem to have passed into a region where you are subject to slightly different laws. New experiences seem to be thrusting themselves under your nose. These periods are so important because we accept a static existence; the heroes of Chekhov and Beckett seem to be saying: 'Things don't change. Things *can't* change. Life just goes on repeating itself, like a gramophone stuck in a groove, and we just get older and die. . . .' But any young man who has just discovered poetry or music or science knows this is untrue. The universe is endlessly new and fresh. And if we find it difficult to be endlessly new and fresh, this is because of some absurd misunderstanding, some piece of ignorance—for example, like a man who took a bath every morning in the same dirty water, unaware that the plug is for empting the bath and the taps for refilling it with clean water. . . .

Being static has its uses. There are periods when the mind *needs* to be closed to outside influences. When I read Freud or Bertrand Russell, I realise that their positive qualities depend on their rather narrow pragmatic attitudes. You cannot bake a cake with the oven door open. Too much open-mindedness makes for mediocrity. We know this instinctively; this is why we accept a certain narrowness of consciousness without too much protest. All the same, it is an exciting moment when mental barriers seem to be withdrawn; the shutters open; light comes in. A chrysalis must feel rather the same as it changes into a butterfly. In such states, you tend to feel sorry for Chekhov and Beckett, and also rather contemptuous; their gloom is largely their own fault.

Arthur Guirdham went into his 'bridge period' comparatively late in life. He specifies the period as his late forties, when he began relaxation exercises. These sometimes produced a sense of being detached from his body or looking down on himself from near the ceiling, but he is careful to state that it was only a 'sense'—not a full-fledged experience. Then there were the cases of clairvoyance, telepathy and healing that he mentions in *Silent Union*. 'Sometimes I acquired the symptoms, often physical, of patients who began to recover at the same time that I had assumed their symptoms. During these periods I experienced all manner of so-called coincidences. People I had never seen for years came vividly to my mind. In a few minutes I would meet them in the street. I would puzzle my mind with abstruse problems. The answers would be provided by strangers I had met in casual encounters. I obtained from these experiences an utter conviction of the indivisibility of human consciousness. I discovered that in the sphere of medicine we share a common psychic life and exchange, with those on the same wavelength, not only thoughts and feelings, but the syndromes of disease.' The ground was being prepared for the insights into Catharism.

The interesting thing is that he was not entirely unprepared; in childhood, and again in early manhood, there had been 'glimpses.' At the age of four, he had a serious illness, and had a dream of heaven—a dream of such intensity that he now believes it to have been a real experience of 'the other world.' He was in a field with a little girl, but the colours had an extraordinary intensity. In his teens, he had experiences of premonitions, none of them important, of things that he would later see in the newspapers; this sounds like the 'time experiences' described by J. W. Dunne. There was also a curious episode in his third year at Oxford. Staying a night at an inn at Beckley, on the edge of Otmoor, he began to shiver violently. A doctor diagnosed a liver complaint. For two days he felt cold and jaundiced, then recovered. Later on, he discovered that Otmoor was one of the last places in England where malaria occurred, and it struck him that he had experienced all the symptoms of malaria, without actually having the disease. It seems to have been a case of picking up the psychic vibrations.

All these speculations about the origins of disease are gathered together and explored in a book called *Obsession* (1972). Here he suggests openly that children's 'night terrors' may not be due to nightmares, but to genuine forces of evil. In an autobiographical book, *A Foot in Both Worlds* (due for publication shortly), he describes one of his own 'night terrors' at the age of six—what seemed to be an encounter with the Devil. In *Obsession,* he is concerned with 'compulsives.' One child patient suffered from convulsions, asthma and night terrors. He was also incredibly, rigidly punctual. He had a recurring dream in which he was gasping with thirst in a desert. He was an omnivorous reader, but never read fiction; he preferred books on Roman history, and on travels in America and Australia—both countries with large tracts of desert, as Guirdham points out. He does not reach any positive conclusions about the patient, but anyone who has read his other books can see the direction of his thoughts: that the deep interest in Roman history could indicate reincarnation, and that the gasping for breath and the dreams of dying of thirst in the desert could stem from an experience in a previous existence. As to the obsessive punctuality, it is the attempt to escape fears 'outside time' by plunging into time—trying to grasp it, so to speak.

He also mentions some cases—which he described to me personally—of houses that produce mental illness; when the patient moves, he tends to recover. He told me of a street in Bath in which thirteen of forty houses have produced mental illness in patients. Here, obviously, we are back to the L-fields and T-fields discussed earlier in this book.

Why am I discussing Arthur Guirdham at such length, when he himself says he is not particularly 'psychic'—only a 'catalyst'? Because I think I can enter into his mind more fully than into that of Robert Leftwich or Mrs. Beattie. For the first fifty years of his life, he was apparently non-psychic. If I had met him twenty years ago, I very much doubt whether I would have predicted that he might become so involved in psychic matters. Why? Because—and here I must tread carefully—I am inclined to believe that 'psychic' activities are often an outlet for energies that could find a more normal creative release. Is it entirely coincidence that Crowley was not a very good poet or novelist? Or that so many people on the fringe of 'occultism' have a highly developed desire for attention and recognition? On the other hand, Guirdham was a successful medical man, Senior Consultant for his area, medical correspondent for a major newspaper. Moreover, he is a naturally good writer. When he sent me his novel *The Gibbet and the Cross,* I expected it to be a typical 'amateur novel,' even though his other books are well written; fiction and non-fiction call for entirely different talents. I was surprised and impressed by the tight, clean prose, the economy, the sense of knowing exactly where he is going. Crowley's novels reveal his mind: sloppy, self-indulgent, undisciplined. Before a man has learned how to make use of his powers, he's always a bit of a confidence trickster; you can smell it in his work. Guirdham has the economy of a man who has learned the trick of creation. You feel you are in the hands of an honest and single-minded man.

So whether or not he he himself possesses 'strange powers,' the issues he raises are perhaps the the most important in this volume. One of the chief drawbacks to most manifestations of 'the occult'—whether in witchcraft, astral projection, communication with the dead—is that they are ultimately *ambiguous.* If the 'spirits' really wanted to convince us of their existence, they could make a far better job of it. Apart from a few really gifted mediums—like Daniel Dunglas Home —or 'magicians,' like Gurdjieff, most 'psychics' raise more doubts than they allay. Name almost any important figure of 'occultism,' from Cornelius Agrippa to Madame Blavatsky, and the suggestions of genuine powers and of charlatanism just about balance one another out.

Now Arthur Guirdham, a man whom no one has so far accused of charlatanism, has made claims that seem to be as startling and far-reaching as those in Einstein's original paper on relativity. His first book on reincarnation could be dismissed by the sceptic as a piece of gullibility; Mrs. Smith happened to engage his intellectual interest with her revelations about Catharism, and he allowed her to convince him that she and he had been associated in the thirteenth century. . . . The second book is not open to this interpretation. It states that half a dozen people, already in loose contact, independently reached the conclusion that they belonged to the Montségur Cathars. The evidence presented is too detailed to be dismissed as self-deception. This is either deliberate, carefully planned deception, or it is an important breakthrough in our knowledge of the universe. If Guirdham is right, then the psychic laws governing human existence are more complex than Darwin or Mendel ever suspected, and the inter-relations between human beings are deeper than Freud ever suspected.

And what do I personally think? My own natural scepticism leads me to wonder if there are not other possible explanations. I must confess that I am basically dubious about Guirdham's dualism. All my life I have been naturally and instinctively a Platonist. That is to say, I have never been able to accept the idea of evil as an independent force; rather, as the outcome of muddle and stupidity. If a moth flies into a candle flame, no evil is involved; no doubt at the next stage in their evolution, moths will learn to develop a sensitivity to heat that will save them from getting singed. A human being who 'commits evil' is one who, for reasons of frustration and impatience, prefers to increase the muddle and chaos in the universe. I do not mind using the word 'evil' about a man who takes pleasure in inflicting pain, for I believe in the existence of free will and of choice; but it still seems to me that he is doing evil out of a kind of inner-muddle. All high-dominance people are possessed by the urge to *do* something, and if they can see no way to create, then they may destroy out of a kind of childish anger with the universe. It seems to me quite possible—indeed, very probable—that the psychic forces of evil unleashed by human beings may persist after their death, so that a house in which someone has been thoroughly miserable or died horribly may retain the imprint for years afterwards. I am even prepared to admit that such 'forces' might behave like discarnate entities, continuing to try to destroy. But that is still a long way from accepting the Cathar position of evil as a genuinely independent force. Moreover, from Guirdham's books, I am not really clear whether *he* is a genuine dualist—that is, one who believes that the world of matter was created by the Devil.* The Church persecuted Manichees and other dualists because the Book of Genesis states that God looked upon the world and saw that it was good; and the basic vision of the mystics has confirmed this. It asserts that the world is a thousand times more beautiful than our senses tell us, and that our habit of 'cutting out' 99 per cent of our experience—which has enabled us to evolve to our present stage—has also prevented us from realising how entirely blessed it is to be alive. If I am honest with myself, I have to admit that I do not have any sympathy for Catharism. The manner in which the Church stamped it out was horrible and wicked; but doctrinally, I suspect I am on the side of the Church.

But then, it does not seem to me that the basic atti-

---

* I am, in fact, a complete dualist. A.G.

tudes of Guirdham's books, from *A Theory of Disease* to *We Are One Another* and *Obsession,* are founded on a dualist point of view. On the contrary, the delight that emerges from his descriptions of nature makes it clear that, emotionally anyway, he looks upon the world and finds it good. His previous incarnation, Roger Isarn, evidently felt the same way, since he lived with 'Puerilia' as his mistress—although he later became a parfait, and presumably renounced sexual pleasure.

At this point, I must squarely answer a question that must have occurred to every reader with a logical turn of mind. In *The Outsider,* I quoted Sartre on this matter of belief. If the telephone rang, and a voice on the other end said, 'This is God speaking. Believe and you are saved; disbelieve and you are damned,' a sensible human being would reply, 'All right, I'm damned.' Even the Bible recommends us to prove everything, and hold fast to what is good.

Now, should I not, according to that formula, totally reject all the claims of Robert Leftwich, Eunice Beattie and Arthur Guirdham—especially Guirdham, since, of the three, he offers least corroboration? Am I not flying in the face of a basic existentialist principle—in fact, a basic philosophical principle?

This is a question that can only be answered in the manner Newman answered Charles Kingsley's accusations of religious dishonesty: by trying to 'explain myself.'

As a child, I accepted spiritualism. My grandmother was a spiritualist. My mother accepted spiritualism, although she never, as far as I know, attended a spiritualist church. I personally have always had a natural distaste for churches and people worshipping together;

for some reason, it arouses in me the same irritable rejection that Einstein always felt when he saw marching soldiers. The whole 'outsider' idea is profoundly ingrained in me (as, indeed, it is in Guirdham—hence his emphasis on the Herd-Personality Impulse). I feel that, ideally, every human being ought to be strong enough to stand totally alone; it is the only way to the realisation of our profoundest capacities. So although I accepted the notion of life after death, the whole idea of a spiritualist church was distasteful to me. But I read books like Harry Price's *Search for Truth* and Conan Doyle's *Wanderings of a Spiritualist*. I once even attempted to read Swedenborg's *True Christian Religion,* but concluded he was feeble-minded.

My spiritualist phase lasted until I was ten or eleven; then I fell in love with science. I use the phrase deliberately, because that is what it was: a love affair, an absorbing passion, a glimpse of salvation. The original impulse came from a book called *The Marvels and Mysteries of Science,* and a cheap chemistry set my mother bought me for Christmas when I was eleven. If Guirdham is right about reincarnation, I think I must have been a scientist in a previous existence. I read Holmyard's *School Chemistry* from beginning to end like a novel, then went on to books like Eddington's *Nature of the Physical World* and Jeans's *Mysterious Universe*. It was a marvellous feeling. Boredom was at an end. No more over-long school holidays in which I wondered what to do, no more hours of listlessly re-reading tattered comics or wondering how I could raise the money to go to the cinema. I had an interest that stayed with me from the time I opened my eyes in the morning until I went to bed at night.

The odd thing is that this passion for science, which led me to write a six-volume *Manual of General Sci-*

ence at the age of thirteen, soon spread to other subjects. I read Joad's *Guide to Philosophy* and *The Concise Cambridge History of English Literature* and Robert O. Ballou's *Bible of the World*. A book on ballet by Arnold Haskell convinced me for a time that I wanted to be a dancer. By the age of sixteen, I felt that science was too narrow; I now read histories of art and music with the same avidity that I had read Holmyard's *Chemistry*. But the interest in spiritualism and the occult had gone completely into abeyance. It was *facts* that interested me. Like Eliot, I felt strongly that 'human kind cannot bear very much reality,' that most people never escape beyond the narrow horizon of the personal and the subjective. Spiritualism struck me simply as wishful thinking. It was too personal—all tied up with people and their emotions and their desire to cling to the past. It seemed to me that the universe is bigger and colder and stranger, and that it doesn't care much about people or their emotions. The only way to evolve is to become more like the universe, to try to be less 'personal.'

I became an obsessive. Not only because of this craving for every possible sort of knowledge, but because I was afraid I might spend the rest of my life working at jobs I hated. This is something Arthur Guirdham and Robert Leftwich might find it difficult to conceive—although Mrs. Beattie wouldn't: the feeling that it may be as hard to escape into a more rewarding, more creative way of life as to escape from Sing Sing. I had no qualifications; when I left school, all I could do was to offer myself as unskilled labour, at the equivalent of ten new pence an hour. Becoming a writer offered the only chance of escape. So I ground away: at stories, at my novel, at essays on Shaw, Nijinsky, Hemingway. . . .

To become an obsessive is to develop a kind of armour, like a crab. The armour insulates you and protects you. It also imprisons you. When you sunbathe on the beach, you can take off your clothes, but not your armour. But then, a prison can also be a useful place, if you have a lot of work you want to get done without interruption. . . .

When an obsessional pattern is established, you get so used to living with inner-tension that you find it impossible to relax. I could only truly relax by inducing a state of wider consciousness through poetry or music. I once sat cross-legged at the top of a small mountain in the Lake District, trying to make myself see Grasmere as Wordsworth saw it; but it didn't work; the relaxation wouldn't come. It felt like a kind of inner constipation.

When *The Outsider* was a success, I knew I could make some kind of a living from writing. I moved to the country. But the relaxation still wouldn't come. Not immediately, anyway. It only came very slowly, taking about five years. I might be looking out of a window as it rained; and suddenly the rain would seem to be falling into my mind. T. E. Lawrence described being taken through an Arab palace; the walls of each room contained a different perfume, which his guide professed to be able to smell. Finally, the guide took him to a room with broken windows, through which the 'cold, eddyless wind of the desert' could blow freely. He said: 'But this is the sweetest smell of all.' Lawrence understood this; but he died before he had learned to relax enough to *experience* it. But I now began to experience it; there were odd moments when my windows opened, and the wind blew in.

I was thirty when Joy presented me with a daughter, and I discovered I could wake her up by thinking about her in the middle of the night, or by looking out of the window when she was asleep in her pram. And the first time I held her, I had a strong sense that she *knew* I was her father. Suddenly, I could understand what it would be like to be a fish, with nerves along your sides that register the pressure of the water, or the approach of an enemy. One day, tired after mowing the lawn, I was about to drop heavily onto the bed and pull off my shoes. Something made me look round; Sally was lying near the edge of the bed; my weight would probably have broken her ribs.

My first child had been born when I was twenty, but there had been no telepathic link; I was still in my carapace—as, I think, Arthur Guirdham's professional duties obliged him to stay in his carapace until he came close to retirement.

In the mid-sixties, I made one interesting and basic discovery: that an immense effort of will serves exactly the same purpose as total relaxation, and achieves it rather more efficiently. In 1966, on my way to America —and a twelve-week lecture tour—I was feeling low and depressed. As the train passed a spot where, twelve years earlier, I had experienced a powerful surge of insight, I suddenly felt a kind of rage, a desire to grab my self-pity by the throat and choke it to death. A furious effort of concentration for just about five minutes produced a sense of strength and freedom, which lasted for most of the tour. But as soon as sheer fatigue began to affect me, after ten weeks of non-stop flying and talking, I became accident-prone; everything began to go wrong. . . .

And in New York in 1967, I noticed the reverse. Paramount had taken an option on one of my novels for a fairly large sum, and I intended to use some of it to take my family to the University of Seattle, where I had a job as writer in residence. But as the date for

leaving England approached, there was still no contract. Half a dozen film deals had already fallen
through; I found it hard to believe that this one would
come off. But although the consequences would have
been fairly serious if the deal *had* fallen through—we
didn't have enough money to get from New York to
Seattle—I declined to allow myself to worry. Staying
with friends on Long Island, I rang my American agent
—who told me that the contracts had been sent weeks
ago. Some incompetent underling had sent them surface mail instead of airmail, and they were probably
halfway across the Atlantic. I still declined to allow
myself to get depressed—it is the writer's occupational
disease, and I have always tried to bully myself out of
it. The next day, my agent rang back to say that he had
got a new set of contracts, and Paramount had agreed
to pay up the moment he handed them over. I set out
from Long Island on an August afternoon; the heat in
the train to Manhattan was almost unbearable; but I
was feeling cheerful. Although Penn Station was
crowded, I managed to get a taxi immediately. Half an
hour later, I signed the contract; my agent said he'd
try to get the cheque to me within forty-eight hours. I
left the office, found another empty taxi outside, arrived
at Penn Station five minutes before the next train out
to Long Island, and was back home within a couple of
hours. There was a strange, sleepwalking sense of
smoothness about that whole afternoon.

Chance? Of course, in a sense. But I also felt that a
kind of alertness and attention was allowing me to
take advantage of chance. It was like being in a canoe
on a fast current; the paddle doesn't have much to do,
but its occasional strokes keep you clear of rocks.

Human beings have a deeply ingrained habit of passivity, which is strengthened by the relatively long

period that we spend under the control of parents and schoolmasters. Moments of intensity are also moments of power and control; yet we have so little understanding of this that we wait passively for some chance to galvanise the muscles that created the intensity.

But whether you use the negative method of relaxation (which is fundamentally 'transcendental meditation') or the positive method of intense alertness and concentration, the result is the same: a realisation of the enormous vistas of reality that lie outside our normal range of awareness. You recognise that the chief obstacle to such awareness is that we don't *need* it to get through an ordinary working day. I can make do fairly well with a narrow awareness and a moderate amount of vital energy. I have 'peak experiences' when I occasionally develop more awareness and more energy than I need for the task in hand; then I 'overflow,' and realise, for a dazzled moment, what a fascinating universe I actually inhabit. It is significant that Maslow's 'peakers' were not daydreaming romantics, but healthy, practical people. . . .

That is my 'general theory.' My increasing sense of the vistas of reality that lie outside my everyday preoccupations leads me to take a far more tolerant attitude towards assertions that do not fit into my range of experience. The cybernetician David Foster came up with an interesting theory (which I described in *The Occult*) to the effect that the universe shows every sign of being run on a series of 'cybernetic codes.' A kind of plastic biscuit with holes in the edge codes my wife's washing machine; and an acorn is the plastic biscuit that codes an oak tree. This suggests to Dr. Foster that acorns and human genes are coded by some conscious intelligence, not simply by the operation of Darwinian selection. He thinks that cosmic rays would be of sufficiently high frequency to do the coding—although this doesn't prove that they do. Now, I don't know whether David Foster is right. All I *can* say is that there is something about his theory that corresponds to my own glimpses of 'vistas of reality.'

Neither do I know whether Robert Leftwich and Eunice Beattie and Arthur Guirdham are right—exactly and precisely right. Mrs. Beattie says that her own insights suggest that reincarnation is not a fact; Guirdham says it is. . . . But it seems to me that they *are* indicating facts that lie outside our present sphere of acceptance. Becher and Stahl were not right when they suggested that all burning materials give off a gas called phlogiston; Descartes wasn't right when he suggested that the movements of the solar system are due to 'vortices.' But they were moving in the right direction; they were recognising the existence of a problem that had so far been overlooked, or only partially recognised. Science has a nasty habit of declining to recognise the existence of problems that lie outside its accepted field; this, I suspect, is due to tidiness rather than fear of the unknown. So the first task of an original thinker is to persuade scientists—or philosophers—that a problem *does* exist. When Freud tried to introduce his ideas on hysteria to the Medical Society of Vienna, their first line of defence was to deny that such a thing as male hysteria existed; Freud had to produce a male hysteric before he could even get them to listen. Even then, the Society found it impossible to fit his theories into their own general system and so decided to ignore them. This is the usual way such things operate, and it is to be expected.

Charles Fort was particularly concerned with this problem. What he wanted to indicate, in four indigestible and impossible books, was that science keeps mistaking its own temporary theoretical boundaries for absolute limits. It is one thing to learn to ignore extraneous noises when you are working; it is another to become so accustomed to ignoring them that you finally deny that they exist. Fort never made his point. By collecting hundreds of odd occurrences from newspapers and printing them all side by side—fishes falling from the sky, skeletons of angels, devil tracks walking over snow-covered rooftops—he only convinced any scientist who happened to open *The Book of the Damned* that he was infinitely gullible. Fort lacked the philosophical training to make his point. It is only nowadays that scientists like Karl Popper, Michael Polanyi, Abraham Maslow, are beginning to make it in a way that scientists can understand.

And even they have only widened the boundaries of scientific tolerance. They have not really made Fort's point: that science often operates in a kind of self-imposed blindness.

Beyond all doubt, things are changing. In the nineteenth century, science *had* to operate that way; the aggressive materialism and doubt were a part of its strength. What good would it have done if someone had recognised that Baron Von Reichenbach was right, and that the human body has some kind of electrical 'aura' or force? This piece of information would have been useless; and it might have hindered Freud in his important work of gaining general recognition for the role of the sex impulse and the subconscious mind. Now, in the light of what we are beginning to learn about the body's 'life fields,' and the way they fluctuate with illness, it could suddenly become as relevant as the sexual theory was in 1900.

In the mid-1960s, the San Francisco writer Dick

Roberts told me that his plants grew better when he talked to them and touched them. I wasn't sceptical, but I pigeonholed this piece of information because I had no use for it. (To begin with, I am no gardener.) Some time later—perhaps a year—my wife read out to me an item from a newspaper asserting that a horticulturist had discovered that plants respond to sympathy. Again, I pigeonholed the information. A few months ago, I read in a book called *Supernature,* by the zoologist Lyall Watson, an account of an experiment that suddenly offered me the general background to Dick Roberts' observation. In 1966, an expert on lie detectors—polygraphs—called Cleve Backster found himself wondering whether a plant would show increased electrical activity when subjected to pain. A lie detector works partly on the change in the electrical resistance of the skin when a man begins to sweat. Backster attached the polygraph to the leaf of a rubber plant in the office, and tried dipping another leaf in hot coffee. The plant didn't register. Backster wondered whether he would get some result by burning the leaf with a match. As soon as he *thought* this idea, the polygraph registered an increase in 'perspiration.' The plant had read his mind. He tried dropping live shrimps into boiling water next to the plant; as each shrimp died in agony, the polygraph needle leapt. When a dead shrimp was dropped into the water, nothing happened.

Another plant, a philodendron, became attached to Backster. Backster's assistant had to produce the various shock responses on the plant, with the result that it would register alarm when he came into the room, and relax when Backster came in—or even when it could hear his voice in the next room. But it was not simply the voice it responded to. Surrounded by a lead screen that would cut out normal electromagnetic vibrations, it still responded. Obviously, these 'vibrations' are not magnetic or electrical.

Watson also mentioned, in an interview published in the *Guardian* (21 September 1973) that he and Backster had tried the same experiment with eggs. When eggs were dropped on the floor or fed to a dog, another egg attached to the polygraph recorded a reaction. This was strongest when eggs were dropped into boiling water. Oddly enough, when this happened, the egg connected to the polygraph ceased to react for several minutes, then would react again as before; Watson's explanation for this is that the egg *fainted* with shock.

I cannot resist mentioning perhaps the weirdest thing in Watson's book. A Frenchman named Bovis who took refuge in the pharaoh's chamber of the Great Pyramid noticed that old litter thrown there—including a dead cat—*did not decay*. This led to the amazing discovery that a cardboard pyramid, built to exactly the same proportions as the Great Pyramid, has the same preservative effect. A dead mouse kept in it 'mummified' without stinking; a similar mouse kept in a shoebox stank. But the strangest thing is yet to come. Razor blades kept in the pyramid remained sharp if they were kept in an east-west alignment. Watson has tried it—he shaved with the same blade for four months without it getting blunt. A Czech firm has actually patented this device. Watson's guess is that the pyramid may build up a magnetic field that causes a new crystalline 'edge' to form on the blade.

Observations like these—which have been confirmed in other laboratories (Watson quotes sources)—obviously lend new perspective to Dick Roberts's assertion that he can influence his plants by talking to them. But it also confirms the general attitude to 'the occult' that

I have argued in this book. I do not know whether Guirdham is right when he says that children's night fears may be due to discarnate entities. But if a plant can sense hostile thoughts, then it is probable that a baby can. And if thought is carried like radio waves, then the 'psychic ether' of our world is probably buzzing with hostile vibrations that a baby might pick up.

Again, Guirdham's title *We Are One Another* takes on new meaning—or perhaps I should say, takes on meaning, for at first sight, it is meaningless. We are *not* one another. On the other hand, the basic assertion of his book is that there are deep psychic links between the Cathars who died at Montségur, so that events in the psyche of one of them could reverberate in the mind of another member of the group who was a total stranger. Many husbands and wives experience each other's illness symptoms. (I mention in *The Occult* that I have experienced Joy's pregnancy pangs and been depressed by her toothache, before I knew she was suffering from it. I once vomited all night when my first wife was suffering from food poisoning a hundred miles away.) Guirdham claims that members of his group of reincarnated Cathars also experienced one another's spiritual crises in the form of spells of dizziness. Naturally, we are sceptical about this, for it contradicts our experience that our inner-worlds are strictly private. But we go on from there to assume that this applies to all nature. And if Backster is right, this is untrue; human beings are the *exception* to the rest of nature. In his essay *The Child in the House*, Walter Pater talks about the 'web of pain' that stretches throughout nature; I remember being deeply struck by the phrase when I read the essay at fourteen or so. But if a rubber plant shudders when a shrimp dies, the 'web of pain' may be more than a poetic phrase.

Again, I was struck when the painter William Arkle

told me how the snakes in his garden seemed to respond to his thoughts. He bought himself a huge house—it used to be a monastery—on a hilltop overlooking Weston-super-Mare. The garden turned out to be full of adders and grass snakes. One adder made a habit of wandering along beside Bill Arkle when he walked down the drive. He had found it coiled in the middle of the drive one day, in such a position that he couldn't drive the car past without killing it. He got out of the car and prodded it awake with a stick; it hissed and declined to move. He decided that perhaps he had better kill it, in case it bit one of the children; as soon as he moved towards it with this intention, it hissed violently at him. Being by nature a gentle mystic, he decided to let it live; the snake immediately moved to the side of the driveway, and went back to sleep. All he told me made it quite clear that the thing was telepathic. Again, I pigeonholed the information. But clearly, it fits. All the indications are that the poets were right when they talked about 'living nature.' And Tolkien's forest that hates hatchets may turn out to be more than a piece of whimsical fiction. All living things exist in a kind of unity that is broken by thought, the need to concentrate on particulars. We exist in a kind of 'psychic ether' of which we are unaware. . . .

All of this certainly lends support to Guirdham's basic theories, although it does nothing to either prove or disprove his belief that a group of thirteenth-century Cathars have been reincarnated in twentieth-century England. All that can be said is that the case he presents in his two Cathar books is the most challenging ever presented. It offers itself for examination. Morey Bernstein's case for the reincarnation of a Colorado housewife collapsed as soon as the Hearst newspapers began to probe it; it turned out that the reincarnated Bridey Murphy had lived opposite an Irishwoman in Chicago as a child, and been in love with her son; the 'memories' of a former existence dredged up from Mrs. Virginia Tighe's subconscious under hypnosis turned out to be childhood memories of her Irish neighbour. But Guirdham's arguments do not depend upon anything as ambiguous as hypnosis. And there were several people involved. This could be the opportunity for the most thorough and exhaustive examination of the case for reincarnation ever conducted. And if the results of such an investigation proved to be positive, then Miss Mills's 'instructors' would have achieved their aim: of making their case known to the widest possible audience. It would be a milestone in the history of psychical research.

Yet the really important change has already taken place. On my desk, as I write, I have two books that I acquired in the last couple of days. One is called *Thirty Years Among the Dead,* by Carl A. Wickland, M.D., published in America in 1924 by the National Psychological Institute. The other is *The Cosmic Clocks,* by Michel Gauquelin, published by the Henry Regnery Company in 1967. The interesting thing is that both books approach their subject from a scientific point of view; Dr. Wickland states that he only intends to present the records and deductions of thirty years' experimental research in the science of normal and abnormal psychology, and within the first few pages he discusses the fascinating case of Sally Beauchamp, the girl with four distinct personalities, recorded by Morton Prince. (I have discussed it in *The Occult.*) But he starts Chapter One: 'The reality of an invisible world surrounding the physical world is for many difficult to comprehend, since the mind sphere is often limited to the visible and tangible; however, it requires but little thought to realise the constant change of matter as it occurs in three forms, solid, liquid and gaseous, in its range back and forth

between the visible and the invisible. . . .' And so on:
'. . . Considering the wonderful advancement of science
into the field of nature's finer forces, it is inconceivable
that any thinking mind can fail to recognise the rationale
of the independent existence of the human spirit apart
for [*sic*] the physical body.' This writing is basically
gobbledegook. The book may or may not be valueless;
but it will certainly convince no one but the converted.

On the other hand, Gauquelin's study deals with bio-
logical clocks, how animals and plants know the time of
day, and kindred subjects. Opening it at random, I find
in Chapter Eleven:

'Around 1950, as we were preparing our critique of
traditional astrology, we found ourselves confronted,
somewhat unwillingly, with a strange result. In one of
our research samples—composed of the birth dates of
576 members of the French Academy of Medicine—the
frequency of the position of certain planets was altogether unusual. The phenomenon did not correspond to
any of the traditional laws of astrology, but it was interesting, nevertheless. What we had observed was that a
large number of future great physicians were born when
the planets Mars and Saturn had just risen or culminated
in the sky. . . .' He goes on to describe how he took a
second sample of 508 physicians—a long job, since the
actual hour of birth is not included in most reference
books—and again discovered that most of them were
born after the rise or the culmination of Mars and
Saturn.

One can sense the whole world of difference between
the two extracts quoted. One is by a spiritualist who is
determined to sound like a scientist; one is by a scientist
who finds himself trying to explain facts that so far have
no place in the framework of science. Gauquelin goes
on to produce various hypotheses about the influence of

'cosmic clocks' on our physical make-up. I do not know whether he is a better scientist than Dr. Wickland, or whether he is more reliable. All I know is that he is treating his subject matter like a traditional scientist. This is how Rutherford and his colleagues worked when it was a question of exploring the 'invisible' realm of the inside of the atom; the facts are taken into account, hypotheses are constructed to fit them, and then research is undertaken to try to uncover more facts, to confirm or deny the theories.

The 'occult' has not yet qualified for recognition as a science. But the day when occultists and spiritualists had to plead to be taken seriously is past. Certain facts are lying around where scientists cannot help tripping over them. And that is a situation which the tidy mind of the scientist finds intolerable. As Charles Fort might have expressed it: If the occult did not exist, science would be compelled to invent it.

About the Author

COLIN WILSON was born in Leicester, England, in 1931, the son of a boot and shoe worker. He left school at 16 and for eight years worked at a series of jobs in factories and on farms. His original ambition to become an atomic physicist was dropped when he left school and his interest shifted to literature and philosophy. His first book, *The Outsider,* published when he was 24, brought him overnight fame and was translated into 20 languages. He has written many other books and has lectured in Germany, Scandinavia and America. Publication of *The Occult* in 1970 led to the formation of a Colin Wilson Society in London, dedicated to developing in man the new faculty, Faculty X, discussed in the book. Wilson lives in Cornwall with his wife and three children.